Contents

DELIVERING
THE MALE

Introduction

A Personal Note

This book owes most to the woman in my life. For twenty-six years I enjoyed the privilege of being husband to Myra, who before her untimely death in 1979 taught me —not always without pain—what it was to be a man. In trivial incidents and major episodes during our years together she encouraged and sometimes demanded my growth, educated me out of many of my typically and pathetically masculine attitudes toward myself, toward women, and toward the world at large. Her perseverance in this labor of love was the single most positive influence on liberating me from much of the oppression that accompanies being a male in our culture.

I remember when, prior to our marriage, speaking out of romantic ardor, I said, "You're perfect!"

Eyes blazing, real anger in her voice, she responded, "No, I'm not perfect. I'm just another human being, with a lot of human failings. You better understand that right now. I refuse to let you shove me into that trap of trying to live up to some foolish notion of yours that I'm perfect."

It was like a solar plexus blow. Years later I was to appreciate that with that one strong stand she had moved me from what psychotherapists call "projective love" to "conscious love." The same period brought forth from me the statement "I need you." Her response, delivered in all passion, was "I don't need you." As I reeled from this declaration, she added, "I love you. I want to marry you. I want to have children with you. I desire you passionately. But I don't need you."

Myra was the only person I've met in fifty-one years of life who had never, prior to her early teens, suffered a blow to her self-esteem. When the blows did come, she coped with a maturity that was grounded in a solid estimate of her worth as a person, one responsible for her own life, capable of making decisions and abiding by the consequences, capable of setting goals and making the sacrifices necessary to achieve them.

I'm certain that in the earlier years of our marriage she was dismayed to discover that I was not as strong in myself as she was in herself. She didn't cater to my deficiencies but insisted that I outgrow them. She openly refused to "mother" me, to protect me from confrontation with myself or from the demands of our relationship. "I'm not your mother," she would insist, "and I refuse to mother you." Instead, she was my wife, and gradually I grew up enough to meet her on common ground: as man to woman, husband to wife, father to mother of the eight children we chose to have.

In the mid-sixties a priest, given the task of introducing me as a major speaker to a gathering of about eight hundred persons in the Northwest, spent five minutes talking about Myra and her amazing grace. He concluded a list of her talents and qualities with "Myra did such a good job of educating her husband to be a father/parent that he wrote a book on the subject—*The Head of the Family*—and now many other fathers are learning from it how to parent their own children." Then, with a sigh, he said, "Myra couldn't be with us this evening; she's pregnant with their next child. Since she couldn't fly here, we did the next best thing and invited her husband, Clay. And here he is."

I have always considered that introduction one of the finest given me in over twenty years of public appearances. Whether I was talking on self-esteem, intimacy, marriage, love, sex, parenting, communication, or any other topic, it was Myra who had educated me to most of what I had to offer others.

One month after *The Ikon*, my first novel, appeared, *The Head of the Family* was published. It was a statement of my own ideals about fatherhood and an attempt to encourage men—too many of whom seemed to define their paternal role solely in terms of breadwinning—to take a more active role in the spiritual, emotional, and psychological development of their children. The welcome this non-fiction volume received totally eclipsed the notices given the novel. Requests for articles, lectures, workshops, and seminars led me to deepen my involvement in family life matters. This involvement eventually led to my becoming a practicing psychotherapist and continues to bring me into contact with men and women in all parts of the country, from all walks of life. As a result, I could deal more effectively and on a more intimate level with the persons who sought help from me. If Myra was the major educational force in my life, the men and women who have shared with me their experiences and problems during these last twenty years have also had a significant role.

One of the most persistent of those problems through the years, arising with more frequency with each passing year, could well be described as "the male condition." Sometimes it presented itself in the pained face of the husband who, in unconscious echo of Freud, said, "I don't know what she wants of me." Sometimes it came as the bitter complaint of wives who don't realize how often other women have used the same phrase to me: "He's just another of the children I have to care for, the oldest boy in the family—that's my husband." In either case it was apparent that in all too many homes the male was not only out of touch with his children on any meaningful level but was also losing, if he hadn't already lost, his wife.

What prompts a woman, mother of three children and married to a successful, sexually active man, to engage in a prolonged clandestine affair—complete with candlelight dinners and motel trysts—with an impotent man?

What is behind the fact that about a third of my clients in therapy at any given time are married women whose husbands refuse to join them in their search for a way out of the pain in their relationship and into closer intimacy and greater joy?

Why is it that, in the majority of cases where couples do come together for counseling, the husband is there because the wife has given the ultimatum: counseling or immediate divorce proceedings?

Why is it that two out of three men I see in my practice have come only after a separation or divorce or after the wife has announced she is in love with another man?

Why do so many women tell me, in the office as well as in the course of my travels, that their husbands are sexually listless and emotionally unresponsive? One woman said: "Our lovemaking was never as frequent as I wanted and nothing to put billboards up about, but ever since he had a slight heart attack seven years ago, it's nonexistent. I asked his doctor and he gave his okay, but if I get a bit sexy with him, he reminds me of his 'weak heart,' and that shoves me off." Another said, "I threw the damned television on the floor one night, trying to get him to stop watching it and pay some attention to me and he just asked, 'You getting your period?' "

Why is it that so many men are patronizing and condescending toward the women in their lives while at the same time living in fear of them?

What prompts so many men to resist meeting the women in their lives on the common ground of mutual intimacy? Why, for instance, is it nearly always the woman who is trying to persuade the man to attend a Marriage Encounter, a Marriage Enrichment weekend, a study day, or an evening on marital communications?

Why do so many men in counseling have such difficulty getting in touch with their feelings, while most women move into such an area with straightforward courage?

Such questions, and many others, have intrigued me for some time. The above listing might seem to imply that women are without problems. Obviously that is not so. I've seen my share of couples where the wife is "distancing" herself, is afraid of intimacy. I've met many women who

are responsible for putting a strain on their relationships
with the significant persons in their lives. However, the
past fifteen years have seen hundreds of books and articles,
indeed whole magazines and national organizations,
devoted to the theme of women's liberation, and we are
witnessing not merely a renaissance of the women's movement but a truly new creation of feminine consciousness.
As this particular evolutionary phase (or, as some would
have it, revolution) has been taking place, however, there
has been no equivalent emphasis upon elevating the consciousness of the male.

Agreed, some men have modified their attitudes as a
result of the educative work of the women in their lives.
Agreed, one of the by-products of the women's movement
has been the liberation of some men from their stereotypical roles and conditioned responses. A case might be
made, however, for the fact that it has caused many other
men to distance themselves even further, to pile on more
armor, to isolate themselves yet more.

I am personally convinced that the male is in many
instances suffering a more acute crisis of identity than his
female counterpart. While the bibliography of articles and
books on this topic continues to grow, and while, in some
parts of the country, small discussion groups of men have
been formed, there is no male equivalent to an organization
like NOW, no national magazine for males equivalent to
Ms. focusing solely upon their dilemma, and discussing
their changing role in today's world. Add to this a male's
acculturated reluctance to voice openly his personal confusion, his sense of being "trapped" in his role, his oppression
of himself through patterning his behavior on outmoded
styles of masculine being-in-the-world, and we have some

understanding of why he continues to suffer personal pain and, often enough, to inflict pain on those he loves.

It is my hope that this work will make a contribution toward eliminating that pain for some men. Initially the thoughts contained in these pages were presented in a number of lectures in downtown San Francisco, during a series of "Creative Lunchbreaks" attended mainly by men and women from the business community. Their comments enriched the draft manuscript. That draft was then sent to men and women—married and unmarried—in different parts of the country and different walks of life for their marginal notations and critical comments. From those notations I gleaned many useful insights, for which I publicly thank them. Their feeling that the book was useful to them and would be helpful to others warmed me with a sense that even prior to publication, the work of clarifying my own thoughts on the theme of this book—what it means to be a man in today's world—has been worth the candle.

So, to the woman in my life, Myra, who had so much to do with my own growth as a man in the world, who taught me so much about myself and educated me as a husband; to my children who continue to teach me what a father is; to my friends and clients who have permitted me to share in their own struggles toward maturity as men and women in today's world, I dedicate this book.

Clayton C. Barbeau

Reflection/Discussion Questions

You can make your experience of this book more personal by considering the following questions and the others that appear at the end of each chapter. Reflect on them individually as you read. Discuss them with the men and women in your life, perhaps inviting them to read the book with you. Use the questions as a basis for a discussion group, especially one where the members feel free to answer or not answer any particular question.

1.   What questions most concern you about men (i.e., males) in contemporary society?

2.   Who has taught you the most about the "male role"?

3.   Have you changed your thinking about the male role in the past few years? If so, how?

Chapter 1

Man, Male, or Boy?

It is important to grasp at the outset that when we discuss our being sexed, we are not referring merely to parts of the body, the external genitalia or internal organs, nor to the fact that most men have facial hair and most women do not or that a man's hair seems more readily lost than a woman's or that men and women have different placement of fatty tissue. Our sex is revealed in every one of the billions of cells in our bodies. My big toe is a male big toe; the hair on my head is a male hair. I am sexed throughout my entire being. Until the second month of my fetal life, however, my physical development was androgynous. Only a bit after the second month do our internal organs begin to take form, and it is during our fourth to sixth month in the womb that certain tissues move toward becoming a clitoris or a penis. Fundamentally, all the underlying musculature is the same for male and female, which is one reason why sex change operations are possible.

Despite the fact that I am sexed in every cell of my body and that, if normal, at birth I enter the world, as of one sex rather than the other, I had to be educated into an understanding of my sexuality, as we all did. That education began at the moment of my birth. At that point each of us begins to learn what it means to be a man or a woman and how we are expected to behave toward other persons, whether of our sex or of the other.

Indeed, when a friend calls to announce a baby's birth, declaring that mother and child are doing fine, the first question asked is "What is it: boy or girl?" This is also the first question of the parents. The response to the question "Boy or girl?" sets in motion a whole pattern of relating to that infant. Our education, our conditioning, if you choose, has begun from the moment mother and father welcome us, the way they hold us for the first time, the tone they use in speaking to us. Soon we begin to distinguish between our parents, to sense their mode of relating to each other—as male and female—and to us.

Foremost among researchers into human sexual development and gender identity are Dr. John Money and Anke Ehrhardt. In a major study of children with sexual anomalies—such as hermaphroditism—which required surgical gender changes, they observed that "the ultimate sex role of the patient depended mainly not on the biological criteria" of chromosomal, gonadal, hormonal, internal and external genitalia but on the "postnatal sex of assignment and rearing and the emergent gender identity of the individual." These social and psychological factors, they state, "appeared to be almost irreversibly fixed by age two."[1]

Whether this sense of gender identity truly originates in the parent or in the infant in his or her cognitive development is still under discussion and study; but all experts agree that our sexual identity is firmly fixed very early in life.

The conditioning of the male, then, is well underway in infancy. For example, one study[2] indicates that boy babies are physically caressed, touched, hugged, and rocked more during their first six months of life than girl babies are, but after that are touched less than girls. Indeed, most mothers then begin to discourage boys from seeking physical contact, usually turning the boy child's attention to toys or other objects. Meanwhile, as early as the second day of life, girl babies are talked to and smiled at more often than infant boys. One possible rationale for thus discouraging boy babies from obtaining physical attention and discouraging them from clinging to mother is the belief that boy babies must learn to fend for themselves, "not be dependent," "stand on their own two feet."

More people are discovering that most "male" and "female" traits are not biologically determined at all but are the result of such early conditioning. All the stereotypes of the culture may be brought into play by the surrounding adults. Grandfather buys the little boy a toy gun or boxing gloves for Christmas and gives the little girl a cuddly doll. The little girl finds herself cooed over at being so delicate, "just a doll," and the little boy is called "toughy" and rough-housed as a little "he-man." Very soon the "little man" is told to be "brave" because "big boys don't cry." He is taught that crying is for "sissies," i.e., for his sister or other females, but not for males. He will actively be discouraged from playing with dolls unless they are "GI

Joe" or other comic-book heroes. Should he come home seeking sympathy because Joey down the block has punched him, he will likely be told that he has to "fight his own battles" and, perhaps, to "punch Joey back" if he gets hit again. The message is very clear: "A man doesn't ask for sympathy or help. A man takes care of himself."

Despite some evidence that younger children are socializing with the opposite sex at an earlier age than previously, the young boy generally finds himself still being discouraged from playing at "girls' games" such as "house" or "cooking." If he does have a particular friend who is a girl, he will become aware of sly winks overhead and the adult smirk surrounding the comment: "John has a little girl friend." The implication, of course, is that having a friend of the opposite sex implies more than mere friendship. The genital difference rather than the personal relationship is given prominence. Very rapidly he learns to "go play with the boys."

In playing with the boys he gets his cruelest lessons in growing up male. He learns rapidly that if he is to have the esteem of his male friends, he must not express any fears, he must not cry nor betray any such "sissy behavior." He learns to look down on girls as weaker than himself. Certain manifestations of creativity may also be taboo. "I loved helping my mother in the kitchen," one client said, "preparing food with her, even cleaning up. But I learned very early never to mention this to my chums. Eventually, I felt I was 'odd' in liking kitchen work and so quit helping out." He is not alone. In one family I recently worked with, the boy children were not expected to do the dishes or help with any housecleaning but their own rooms. The girls, however, were expected to help their mother with the "women's work." Through such conditioning processes the boy child learns to avoid expressing sensitivity and to remain ignorant of various domestic and child-care skills.

By the time he enters school, the young boy finds himself in an ambivalent position regarding the opposite sex. He has been told repeatedly that he mustn't hit a girl (though, apparently, it is all right to hit a boy); that girls are weaker than he is; girls are not to have things thrown at them; girls can't play football. In short, girls are fragile, delicate, weak beings in need of a boy's protection and care. At the same time, his life is governed, for the most part, by his mother. Whether his father is absent because of divorce or death or is simply away at his job, or whether (as is often the case) the father simply chooses to spend little time interacting with him, the young boy sees his mother as the one who controls the quality of his life. She is the powerful being who gives or withholds approval, who provides lunch and love. He leaves the authority figure of his mother to go to school, where, despite the increasing frequency of male teachers at the grammar-school level, his first authority figure in the outside, larger society is usually another woman. Competent, grown-up, she likewise has power over his daily happiness or unhappiness. If most principals are still men, such administrators, like his father, are most often distant figures. Direct, daily authority over him is most often exercised by a woman.

The contradictions inherent in this conditioning of the young boy are evident and not easily solved. For some males the dichotomy continues to be a source of ambivalence even into adulthood. As adults, such males vacillate between patronizing the "little woman," insisting on her dependency or childlike status and yet, at the same time,

living in secret fear of her power to make their life misera-
ble. These are the males whose sense of masculine strength
is bought only by the superficial or real dependency evidenced by their wives.

A clear example of this was brought to my attention by a
woman who, when the youngest child entered school,
decided to take some courses herself. Her husband gave
verbal approval, but as the weeks went by she realized a
pattern of sabotage was at work. "He invited his supervisor
to dinner on one of my class evenings. On another, he
needed the car. On another, he notified me at the last
minute that he was staying on at the office, leaving me no
time to find a baby-sitter and a way to class. Of course, I
missed those evenings. When I realized what was happening, I simply no longer fell for his tricks. Then he withdrew. He stopped any lovemaking. He grew sullen. He
hasn't touched me physically in three months. When I
touch him, he shies away. Last week I confronted him on
this and he said, 'Divorce me. You don't need me any
more. Divorce me and do your own thing. I'll keep the
kids. They need me. You don't need me anymore. Go on,
be independent, if you want to. . . .' "

Many males who panic at any show of their wife's
financial or social independence don't manifest it so
clearly. Some merely insist on total control of the purse
strings, keeping their wives in the dark about the family's
financial status. Others vacillate between attempts to live
out the role of "he-man" proffered by the male mystique
and the passive dependency of the little boy.

At some point in his growing up, nearly every male has
had to cope with the competition of the playing field. If

not in impromptu games arranged among the boys themselves, then in Little League or, inevitably, in school, they
find themselves tested. I was a very small boy for my age. I
did not begin to grow tall until late adolescence. I recall
the agony of those childhood days when I was always the
last, or second to last, chosen to play on any team. Sometimes I went, as it were, by default, as the last kid standing
there: "Well, if we gotta take him, we gotta." In baseball I
was inevitably sent to right field, where not too many balls
were hit and where, ostensibly, I wouldn't cost the team
too many runs. Because I was so short I wasn't very good
at basketball either. And because I was skinny I wasn't
much help in football. Since sports are where male toughness is best displayed, where prestige is won among peers
and the school heroes created—idols of cheerleaders and
prize dates for school dances—I learned early on that I was
neither prize hero nor prize date. I doubt that mine was an
isolated experience of boyhood. After all, what percentage
of boys can make the team?

I personally compensated by vicariously participating in
the exploits of fictional heroes, reading everything I could
get my hands on. This led to a certain verbal proficiency
and psychological acumen that came in handy for a small
kid. More than once some bruiser's desire to exercise his
masculine prowess on my obviously puny form was side-
tracked by my skillful use of language. Certainly as time
went on I discovered that girls liked talking with me, and
since they were more scholastically inclined than most boys
were, I got along well with them. However, when the chips
were down they dated the athletes. The most memorable
example of this was the lovely girl who was the light of my
life for a few months. We walked and talked together, did

our homework together. Our idyll ended when she abruptly dropped out of school because she had gotten pregnant as a result of backseat gymnastics with one of the school's athletes.

How powerfully this athletic mystique grips the American male is demonstrated in the fact that one of this country's great literary talents, F. Scott Fitzgerald, in one of his last essays, "The Crack-Up,"[3] lamented the two great sadnesses of his life: that he did not make Princeton's varsity and that he did not get overseas in World War I. The latter point ties in with the former. The playing field is presumably the place where toughness and aggressive behavior, hallmarks of the masculine mystique, can be proven. The other arena, supposedly, is in the life-and-death struggle of the battlefield.

Warren Farrell and Marc Fasteau, among others, have made the point that America's policy of "toughness" in Vietnam was seen as proving the masculinity of its leaders.[4] No one was going to call them "sissy" or make them back away from a fight, no matter how senseless. That this same toughness code remains in force is testified to by the subsequent political fates of Thomas Eagleton, who admitted seeking help for a personal problem, of Edmund Muskie, who actually shed a tear while denouncing a scurrilous attack on his wife, and of George Romney, who confessed a mistake in judgment!

A retired military man came to me seeking counsel for a most painful marital situation. One aspect of the problem was his wife's alcoholism and her bizarre behavior while intoxicated. The other was her increasing paranoia when sober and her demand that they move to another apartment or house—demands he had been meeting about three times a year before coming to see me. He was a career military man, having gone to military academies even in his earliest youth. He had earned more than one man's share of decorations and medals. His initial minutes with me were spent in embarrassed apologies for being there: "You must think I'm a failure. God, I never thought I'd have to ask anyone for help."

I reassured him I didn't think him a failure at all. Quite the contrary, in overcoming the most stringent conditioning in male toughness that the culture has to offer, he had shown great courage. Out of love for himself and his wife he had taken a step that went against all his training. That was heroism. As he told his tale of this domestic combat that had taken a more drastic toll on him than any wartime ordeal, I was studying him intently. When he finished, I asked, "And how do you feel about that?"

His chin firmed, his eyes flashed, his teeth seemed to bite off the words. "I'm mad. I'm goddam angry."

I looked at him and shook my head. "I don't believe you, Colonel. I accept the fact that you believe you at the moment, but I don't. Until I asked that question, your body posture, your eyes, your pulse rate, the way you were breathing, your tone of voice—everything about you said you were really sad, terribly unhappy."

All the tension went out of him, and tears welled into his eyes. "I'm so unhappy I could cry." And then, suddenly aware of the tears, he hurriedly swabbed them away despite my suggestion that he might want to give himself permission to let them flow a bit. He was embarrassed, however, and our final minutes of working together were marred by his constant references to his tears: "I must apologize . . .," "God, never happened to me before. . . ."

As it turned out, he didn't keep his second appointment. Nor was I surprised, for the emotions touched in him during that first session were, from his point of view, signs of weakness. The male mystique of toughing it out, of never showing vulnerability or sensitivity to pain, of never admitting a mistake, is still very much the code among American (and many other) males. With precisely those attitudes most men assuredly oppress themselves.

In the boy child, such attitudes are motivated by the desire to avoid at any cost that awful insult of "sissy." In the grown male, these attitudes are motivated by the horror of being thought a homosexual. I see before me now the tear-streaked face of a high-school classmate whose father, upon learning of his son's ambition, absolutely derided and successfully thwarted the boy's dream of becoming a ballet dancer. No son of his was going to shame him by getting into a "fairy profession." I recall the number of epithets, particularly in college days and in the military, that were used to keep young men part of the male herd, epithets that always implied that deviation from the male code of toughness was a sign of one's being a "queer," a "faggot," or a "fairy." These were the ultimate insults. They were especially favored by drill instructors who wanted to inspire greater enthusiasm during bayonet practice.

The competitive spirit coupled with the fear of homosexuality proves a strong double lock on the male's inner self, especially in his dealings with males. In such dealings he either fears that the other male will use it against him if he reveals himself and his feelings (especially his fears or weaknesses), or else he fears that his very desire for such sharing may be some hidden homosexual prompting. This pattern is changing with the younger generation to some degree, but few males have intimate male friends. The large majority of men remain trapped in their own self-built prisons. In a discussion of this topic at the home of a Stanford University student, a young woman contended she did not think this was as valid for men now in their twenties. Significantly, two men, one a medical resident, disagreed with her. Equally significant, no other men disagreed with their comments.

If the majority of men do not have true friendships with other men, there seem to be just as many who do not share their feelings with their wives. I draw not only upon my own counseling experience but upon the comments of hundreds of women I have met during my lecture tours when I say that one of the most common complaints I hear from wives is that their husbands won't share with them on the emotional level. In counseling I find this silence flows from the husband's fear that his wife will think him weak or unmanly if he voices some self-doubt or gives evidence of some sensitivity of feeling. After all, as protector of the "weaker sex" he must show himself strong, ready to meet any situation, prepared to "tough it out."

One of the anomalies of all this, of course, is that we continue to educate our young males for a world that no longer exists. In later pages we will discuss in more detail how the male's behavior, his tough individualism, his pro-tector role, his physical strength, and even his competitive drive are obsolete or on the way to obsolescence in our time. The corporate structure, the powerful state, the computerized technology which in the main he will claim as his creations have rendered his most prized "masculine" qualities obsolete. Indeed, it may be that the increasing

emphasis on athletic endeavor and the popularity of specta-
tor sports such as football are related to this desire to find
expression somewhere for the outmoded "masculine" attitudes. That some athletes now earn more money than the
leaders of nations only hints at the presumed value of the
service they perform. For vicariously, while watching a
television screen or sitting in the stadium, the male can
participate in the athlete's show of aggressive strength,
identify with one side of a competitive battle, scream out
his epithets, and know the ecstasy of victory or the agony
of defeat.

Which, not strangely, brings us to sex. Not long ago I
remarked to a woman friend that I felt that much of the
powerful orgasmic thrill that some men used to find in
sexual lovemaking is now experienced in watching their
team make a touchdown. Two weeks later, she wrote me a
letter. She said she had observed her husband and his male
friends as they watched a televised football game. Keeping
my remark in mind, she was particularly attentive when
"their side" made a touchdown. She wrote: "You were
right. My husband threw himself back with an explosion
of pleasure greater than any he has seemed to enjoy in sex
since the earliest days of our marriage. The other men
weren't very different."

There is a tie-in, I believe, between the phallic nature of
male sexuality and the aggressive drive. The sexual act
itself cannot take place unless the male takes an active role
and, particularly in the culmination of the act, is to some
degree aggressive. This is not true of the woman, who can
remain passive throughout if she so chooses. (That some
women no longer choose to remain passive is itself bringing tensions into some relationships.) Most males in our

society have been raised to view their sexual ability as part of that same competitive life-style, that same aggressive combat, that tests and defines their maleness. Norman Mailer's story "The Time of Her Time"[5] is but one example. He refers to his penis as an "avenger" and uses violent athletic language, particularly the language of a boxer, in describing his sexual conquest of a young woman. The story concludes with the young woman throwing a taunt at his fear of homosexuality.

Consider, too, the widespread use on the singles scene of "scoring" as a term whereby males talk of having "made" or "laid" some woman. Sexual relations are thrown at the male throughout his youth and early adulthood as the test of his manhood. The quality of his relationship with the girl or woman has no part in such "man talk"; the only important question is whether he "scored" and, in some circles, how often. In his earlier years, the queries might relate only to how "far" he had got or whether he had "struck out."

In my youth it was up to the male to see how far he could get and up to the female to set the limits on how far he would get. This game of escalation was not uncommon in my high-school days. It was a game in which, more often than not, the male was trying to maintain face by at least attempting what he thought his peers and perhaps the girl herself expected of him, and where, as frightened and curious as he, she was trying to keep him as a boyfriend and yet not lose her reputation as a "nice girl." In those days the game led to many early marriages. Today, despite more permissiveness and increasing emphasis on sex education, my talks with high-school groups (in which students get to hand in anonymous written questions) reveal that this game is still being played.

Many males today still think of the sexual act in terms of sheer aggression and conquest. They emphasize performance. For these individuals, "scoring" remains a way of continuously proving to themselves that they are not homosexual, that they are sexually attractive, that they are males. But, as with the successful athletes, each game demands that they again be tested and found adequate. Sooner or later, the male who has reduced sex to this sort of athleticism tires of the game.

In the past fifteen years one of the most interesting phenomena noted by myself and other marriage counselors has been the shift from hearing wives complain that their husbands were too sexually demanding to having wives complain that their husbands show little interest in sexual lovemaking. Part of the reason for this may be the attitude of the men themselves: that each act is in itself an adequacy test. Since sex has been turned into work—with technical manuals included—and has as its product the delivery of an orgasm to the partner, or a simultaneous orgasm or a multiple orgasm, many males simply do not want to put themselves to the test anymore. In some cases I've treated, the male had become non-orgasmic as a result of his performance orientation. Focusing entirely on the delivery of an orgasm to his wife, feeling himself a failure if he did not deliver, he short-circuited his own emotional response. His ejaculation, when it happened, would pass nearly unnoticed on the emotional or psychic level. Typically, these same males had no pattern of receiving pleasure from their wives and were uncomfortable if the woman tried to give a massage or to take the active role in sexual pleasuring. To these men, being the passive partner, receiving, was "feminine."

Today, with more wives feeling freer to express their own sexual needs, especially their need for a sense of emotional connectedness, of intimacy and deep communication of feelings as the foundation for the best sexual experiences, many males retreat. Apparently things were simpler for them when all they had to do was use women as receptacles for their pent-up sperm. The demand for intimacy, for emotional responsiveness in the total relationship, intimidates such males.

The tragedy in this, of course, is that the male is often quite out of touch with his own feelings, has had little, if any, experience in articulating his inner states to himself or to others. His whole upbringing has worked to disconnect him from the tender, sensitive, caring, suffering, needing aspects of his being. If the male mystique has taken firm hold of him, he not only merely hides these things from his fellows; he has great difficulty acknowledging them even to himself. One does not have to be a psychotherapist to know that men have all the capacity for feeling, for laughter and tears, for tenderness and love, all the yearnings for warmth and emotional closeness, all the capacity for spiritual experience and aesthetic delight that women do. But so many men have become wary of disclosing these aspects of their being to anyone else for fear of being thought weak and unmasculine that they have actually lost touch with their own inner life.

Precisely because they have lost touch with themselves, having played the male role so long they believe the mask to be their true face, these males tend to give "objective" responses to emotional situations, to withdraw, get "uptight," become more impersonal even as their wives demand or request or plead for more emotional rapport. Often, in the counseling situation to which they have been brought by the wife threatening divorce, they will counter her statements of emotional neediness by reciting a list of the material things they have worked so hard to get for her.

As Herb Goldberg, Ph.D., points out in *The Hazards of Being Male*:

Emotionally repressed, out of touch with his body, alienated and isolated from other men, terrorized by the fear of failure, afraid to ask for help, thrown out at a moment's notice on the occupational junkpile when all he ever knew was how to work, it is perhaps surprising that the suicide statistics are only what they are. Perhaps, however, the male has become an artist in the creation of hidden ways of killing himself.[6]

Those "hidden ways" include ulcers, heart attacks, high blood pressure, and other stress-induced symptoms.

It is my personal experience that we have altogether too many males in our society (that is, masculine gender human beings) who are still imprisoned in the male mystique, who are oppressing themselves and trying to live up to a code that is dehumanizing to them and to women and is injurious to our whole society.

We have another, though smaller, group of "boys" (that is, human beings of masculine gender) who have never outgrown their passive dependency status and who married Mommy or who, if single, assume a passive attitude toward their own lives. One woman who read this book in its early draft insisted, "I like the distinction you make between men and boys. However, I believe that *all* men marry their mothers, and nearly all married men I know are passive in

their relationships with their wives." Another wrote: "All
that space devoted to the 'male' and so little to the 'boy,'
when it is the multitude of boys in our midst who are in the
majority! Surely most wives seem to be trying, though it is
not their responsibility, to get their husband/boys to
become men. Some would even welcome a 'male' instead
of a 'boy,' if that were the choice."

The "boy" will be discussed in greater detail in our next
chapter. He is the husband who says "I don't care," or
"Whatever you want, honey" to the wife seeking some help
in decision-making. He may be ridiculously insistent that
his children agree with him in inconsequential things, saying "They have no respect" if they don't do so. He is
usually, though not always, sexually less active than his
wife wishes. At work he is considered "a good guy"
because he is "one of the gang," but he is not a leader and
envies the freedom and "devil-may-care" attitude he sees,
however mistakenly, in the others. Married or single, he
sees himself as a victim of circumstances, a person whose
life is made up of "good breaks" or "bad breaks." If
married, he is constantly worried about pleasing his
wife/mother but feels unappreciated by her and by the
children and unknown by anyone on earth.

It was not always thus. His mother loved him, he knows.
And when he met his wife-to-be he saw in her all the
qualities of his mother's nurturing and tender self. His
earliest months in the marriage were, typically, quite
delightful, and he felt he was the luckiest man on earth to
have found so much tenderness, caring, and attention. The
change began when the first child arrived. Usually at this
point the seeds of the male's discontent begin to germinate.
His wife is now obviously somebody else's mother, and she

shows this new person the tenderness and love once entirely his. A new demand for growth is also made upon him now: that he assume new responsibilities, parental ones. He may resent this, consciously or unconsciously. It is not uncommon for him to feel like a "motherless child," deserted, misunderstood, orphaned. He may turn increasingly to his own natural mother for consolation. At his core, often enough, is a ball of anger that he finds frightening and that he suppresses most of the time. This anger finds expression, when it does, in the sort of behavior his wife has seen in the children when they are going through the "terrible twos," i.e., being contrary, yelling, breaking things, sulking. He smiles a lot when he is with people outside the family circle.

I would define men as those persons who, whatever their experiences of the masculine mystique, have chosen to avoid the stereotypical male role *as well as that of the boy.* Having seen fit to take charge of their own lives, they assume responsibility for themselves, their feelings, their personals goals and desires. They seek clarity with themselves, first of all. They tend to be in touch with their own needs and wants. They are willing to express their feelings, will risk themselves in encounters with those around them. Men confront the woman they've married or have just met not as inferior, nor as servant to their needs nor as a potential validation of their manhood or a replacement for mother, but as a unique human being whose mystery is inexhaustible. Men do not experience sexuality as some extension of the football field or battlefield but as a further means of sharing themselves with one they love. A man knows that such sharing in sexual knowledge with another —just as with all self-disclosure or self-gifting—cannot even begin to take place save in a context of trust and mutual caring.

The male world has for too long been structured as a world without tenderness, without sensibility, without caring, without tears, without the freedom to express honest emotions spontaneously. In short, the male world has been a world without love.

The boy's world, by contrast, is structured around the passive dependency of someone unwilling to enter the adult world of accepting responsibility for the creation of his own life, of someone seeking only to be cared for and nourished by the mother figure he married or by anyone else who is willing to assume responsibility (and blame) for his life.

The times demand that our boys grow up to be men. The day has come for males to quit playing the old roles and to take off their masks. The world is crying out for more men willing to take on the responsibilities of men and to engage in the work of men: building up the community of love.

Reflection/Discussion Questions

1. What were your favorite toys and activities as a child? What does that say about your sexual conditioning?

2. Were some options closed to you as a child because of your sex?

3. Can you remember instances where competition and "male toughness" proved destructive to someone's self-image?

4. Have you seen the fear of being thought a homosexual operate in others? in yourself?

5. Does the discussion of our cultural view of sexual activity as a "performance test" ring true to you?

6. How much have you repressed your own emotions throughout your life?

7. Of the men you know well, classify each one as man, male, or boy.

8. If you are a male, what defenses, arguments, resistance do you experience at the thought of putting aside some of the male's armor? If you are a female, how do you react to the idea?

Notes

1. Cited in Saul Rosenzweig, "Human Autonomy as an Evolutionary Attainment, Anticipating Proceptive Sex Choice and Idiodynamic Bisexuality," in *Contemporary Sexual Behavior: Critical Issues in the 1970's,* Joseph Zubin and John Money, eds. (Baltimore and London: Johns Hopkins University Press, 1973), p. 212.

2. Michael Lewis, "Parents and Children: Sex Role Development," *School Review* 80 (1972).

3. F. Scott Fitzgerald, *The Crack-Up*, Edmund Wilson, ed. (New York: New Directions, 1945), p. 70.

4. Marc Fasteau, *The Male Machine* (New York: McGraw-Hill, 1974); Warren Farrell, *The Liberated Man* (New York: Bantam Books, 1975).

5. Norman Mailer, "The Time of Her Time," *Advertisements for Myself* (New York: Signet Books, 1960), pp. 427-451.

6. Herb Goldberg, Ph.D., *The Hazards of Being Male* (New York: Signet Books, 1976), chapter 12.

Chapter 2

The Man-Woman Crisis

In the earliest pages of our scriptures we hear Adam singing the first wedding song: "This is now bone of my bones, and flesh of my flesh: she shall be called Woman." Not very long after that, the same Adam points the finger of blame at this creature of creatures whom he had so rejoiced at discovering and seeks to pin on her the rap for his moral lapse: "The woman whom thou gavest to be with me, she gave me of the tree, and I did eat."

The scriptures of humankind, sacred and secular, ever since have had as one of their major themes the exultant joy of men and women discovering the other who seems to promise an end to loneliness and a beginning to loveliness. Almost as prevalent a theme in literature is the theme of failure, the disillusionment, the misunderstandings and disappointments of the man-woman relationship. There is no lack of record of the triumphs and tragedies of this aspect of human life.

Still, for most of human history and for most of human-kind, the respective roles of men and women have been determined by the needs for maintenance and survival of the family and tribe or nation. Whatever we may think of such roles as they were worked out in different cultures in different eras, the fact is that they were usually clearly defined. In times previous to ours, most men and women conformed to patterns of behavior toward each other that were taught by their society. It was left to our current century—with its newborn industrialism, its rapid shift of population from farms to cities, its sudden access to cross-cultural information, its universal education, its advances in communication and personal mobility—to shatter the old functional roles. Add to the list the new demands of a technological society, the enormous increment of scientific research, the advances in knowledge of human behavior, the provision of means of having sexual pleasure without fear of pregnancy, and we have the elements that dramati-cally render obsolete previously hallowed patterns of the man-woman relationship. Despite this, much of our accul-turation of boys and girls for their adult man-woman roles persists in educating them for patterns of sexual relating that are no longer functional. This cultural lag appears to be a major factor in the current almost palpable tension between men and women in our society. As indicated in the previous chapter, we still tend to educate the majority of boys in modes of behavior that place the masculine label upon toughness, the suppression of tender emotions, the notion of masculine dominance over women. Many a male carries throughout life the ambivalence he was taught. On the one hand, females were supposedly inferior, weaker, more passive creatures whose very dependence upon the male's superior powers helped define his masculinity. On the other hand, the most powerful authority figures in his formative years, persons capable of making him happy or unhappy, were females.

Often enough, the only area in which a particular man can feel or assert his power over women is in the economic sphere. Many men define their roles in family life solely in terms of being the "breadwinner." Thus they are threatened when their wives decide to earn an income of their own, and even some of the most "liberated" men are unwilling to see their wives earn an income larger than their own. More than one professional woman has turned down a job promotion with increased income because it would mean that she would be making more money than her husband and she didn't think he would be able to adjust to that. At the same time, some women who are totally economically dependent upon their husbands have very negative feelings about their own situation. A former client has written me about this:

> I remember the freedom I felt when I got my first paycheck for a part-time job. I had earned this money. I could now buy those things (a new lamp, fix the kitchen floor, etc.) that Peter said we couldn't afford. He was making $34,000 a year. I never could understand why we couldn't afford nicer furniture, etc. It was two months after I took the part-time job that he said he was leaving me to marry another woman (or should I say "mother"?). All I cared about, he said, was a career. He told people I wasn't satisfied with my home life; that it was obvious I was really messed up.

My earning power was very subtly sabotaged. All counseling fees were to be paid by me—"You're the one who wanted this!" Any time we had dinner out other than for social or business reasons, I paid. After all, if I didn't have that job, I wouldn't be too tired on Friday night to make dinner, right?

For many men, not only does economic power continue a superior-inferior notion of the male-female relationship; many men expect it to be understood as an expression of their love. "I don't know what in hell more she can want from me," one client shouted. "She can write a check for any damned thing she needs." His wife was asking for intimacy. She phrased it as "consideration for my feelings," "a willingness to listen to me," "sharing his feelings with me." He countered such declarations with angry assertions of his economic strength, flexing his money muscles. "You ought to see the home I've bought her. And she's got her own car."

The male mystique works in other ways to destroy healthy relationships between men and women. One man had ignored his wife's feelings for years. He had had more than one affair, which, while not overtly boasting about, he made little attempt to conceal from his male friends. His wife confronted him one day with the news that she was getting a divorce in order to marry a man to whom she had turned for intimacy. The husband went on a furniture-breaking rampage, threatened murder, stormed out for a three-week binge, flirted with suicide, then sobered up and promptly moved into the apartment of one of his former bedpartners. He incorporated into that behavior much of the male mystique: He subscribed to the double standard; he threatened aggression against others and himself as a solution to his problem; he then sought out another woman to be dependent upon him, thereby reassuring himself of his masculine power. Informative as is his reaction to the crisis, it is a reaction rooted in the same male mystique that led to his marital breakup.

Another client came in with a typical problem: After eight years of marriage, she was finding her husband's unwillingness to communicate, his lack of feeling, growing more and more intolerable. The more she pressed him toward fuller intimacy, the more he withdrew from her. He had taken to working overtime all the time. He had withdrawn from sexual contact in the weeks preceding her initial appointment for counseling. Significantly, he had refused to accompany her to that appointment. The idea of counseling was even more threatening to him than her requests for self-revelation. Unwilling to let his wife see him as vulnerable, he was not about to announce to some other person his feelings of inadequacy. "His greatest concern right now," she said during the first interview, "is that I'm going to talk about him." Another divorcee who read this wrote me, "Every time I'd speak to a priest, friend, or you, Joe would say, 'What did you say about me? What did he say about me?' He'd grill me about details, fearing I'd tarnish his image." Caught up in the choice of either opening up and thereby growing up in the intimacy required in the marital relationship or else facing a divorce, all too many men choose to "tough it out." Rather than reveal themselves in a counseling situation or otherwise move the relationship onto a more intimate personal level, they choose divorce or are divorced by their wives. Such males often blame the woman's deficiencies for the divorce. Their theme song might well be the refrain from the old popular song: "I'd rather have a paper doll that I can call my own than have a fickle-minded real live girl."

Actually, the couple just described, and another very much like them who came to my attention in recent months, were helped by taking a middle course. Invited to a Marriage Encounter weekend, these couples attended and discovered that other couples had confronted the same sort of crisis in intimacy and through improved communication had found a new freedom and joy, a new way of relaxing. Yet for all too many the crisis of intimacy does not have this sort of happy ending—or rather this happy beginning of a lifetime of mutual discovery. The masculine unwillingness to risk self-disclosure is a major component of the man-woman crisis in our time and is a major cause of divorce in our society.

In April 1977 the Associated Press carried a story stating, "Adultery is the cause of nearly half of the problems that marriage counselors deal with, according to research by the President of the American Association of Marriage and Family Counselors." The article went on to say that "a survey of 100 marriage counselors across the country indicates that 45% of the cases they deal with involve adultery." The report indicated that one-third of the couples planned to divorce "because of the affair."[1] But to say that adultery is the cause of nearly half the problems counselors deal with is like saying that running noses are the cause of nearly half the colds in America, or that a pain in the side is the cause of appendicitis. This is a journalistic confusion of a symptom with a cause.

The symptom of adultery on the part of wives has been, in my counseling experience, most often caused by a searching for intimacy with a man who cares and who demonstrates his caring, for a personal relationship that the husband is not supplying. One woman having an affair with an impotent man stated, "My husband is a stud in bed, but my lover is just that, a romantic lover who listens to me, who shares with me." Adultery on the part of a husband, on the other hand, is often a flight from the very demands of intimacy his wife is making. "She wants too much. I can't take all that closeness," one wandering husband disclosed. Particularly in one-night stands, he finds he can have some sexual activity without love, without self-revelation. And therein he hopes to find reassurance of his masculinity. The very fact that he needs such constant reassurance signals the location of his personal difficulties. The misnamed "great lovers" Don Juan and Casanova were likewise afflicted: Because their last conquest had not proved to them that they were adequate, they had to find another.

In reality, the sexual act itself—and the male orgasmic response—is closely tied to these problems. It is not uncommon for both husbands and wives to express dissatisfaction with their sexual lovemaking: she because of the lack of positive emotional content, of tenderness or true intimacy in their relationship, he because he finds her basic dissatisfaction, or her demands, a hindrance to his sense of "good performance." Her lack of response and his sense of failure often lead to a diminishing, even disappearance, of sexual lovemaking in marriage.

One client, separated for over a year, said, "Initially I begged him for some understanding. He simply tossed a sex manual at me. When I suggested counseling he said no. He said the problem was mine, not his. For the last ten years of our marriage, we lived like good friends, brother and sister, good parents. To the outside world, we were a lovely couple. Then I decided life must offer something more. Our separation was amicable. Then I met a man. He courted me, paid attention, listened, understood, responded to me as a person. When we finally, months later, made love, I discovered there was nothing wrong with me; I loved it. I think it was because he touched me emotionally, spiritually, personally, long before he ever touched me physically."

Because the male tends to think of the sexual act as an adequacy test, a performance equivalent to the strong swing of the hammer that will ring the gong at the state fair, he may not understand the causes of his wife's dissatisfaction. If he is one of those who is focused on "providing" an orgasm for his wife as a means of showing his prowess, he may himself get little pleasure from the activity. And if he fails to "provide" an orgasm, he too is dissatisfied. About 50% of the husbands I have seen in counseling the past three years have echoed the remark of the husband who said, "I just don't get anything out of it. I mean, she comes, but if it weren't for her, I'd not even bother." They are admitting to being nonorgasmic. As Rollo May has pointed out:

> Therapists today rarely have patients exhibiting repression of sex in the old-fashioned sense. . . . In fact we find just the opposite: a great deal of talk about sex, a great deal of sexual activity. . . . But our patients do complain of a lack of feeling and passion; so much sex and so little meaning or even fun in it.[2]

I have been present in group therapy sessions where women, married and single, speak of their difficulties in

coping with men. "I've always got to be careful of his
tender ego," one said. "I'm tired of catering to the tender
egos of men. Gotta supply an orgasm or he's crushed.
Can't contradict him or be too active sexually, or he says
I'm too aggressive. Gotta be careful not to let him see I'm
more up on certain topics than he is, or he'll withdraw from
the discussion. Damn it, I'm tired of nursing male egos."
She was a single woman. Married women say the same
things in different words. I've heard a veritable chorus of
voices saying, "I'm tired of being his mother. I want a
husband. I want a man to husband me, not a big boy who
alternates between boasting to his friends, getting into
angry rages with me or the kids and then coming with
whimpering requests for sex, like it was some sort of candy
I dole out when he's been a good boy for the last hour."

Coupled with complaints that "he's the oldest boy in the
family" and "he won't talk to me of anything that really
matters" (i.e., won't talk of their relationship or what's
really happening with him or them) is the plaint that "he's
more in love with television sports than with me." The
television program "Love American Style" once had a skit
which illustrated this syndrome. The husband was totally
caught up in watching a football game, while the wife tried
every seductive wile she knew to distract him from the
ongoing competition to her presence. Failing every effort,
she finally shouted, "You love football more than you love
me!" He turned for the moment to announce, "Yes, but I
love you more than I love baseball," and returned to watching the game.

Humorous as the sketch was, it is less than humorous
when seen in the life of the women who know its truth. In
my office a weeping wife heard her husband declare, "I'd

give you up before I'd give up golf." One woman, upon reading a news report on an interview with me in Louisiana, wrote me a letter spelling out the pain of having a husband who continually sacrificed her and the family on the altar of his avid interest in televised sports. In such cases it seems apparent that sports are being used merely to avoid intimate contact with the spouse. One athlete whose wife had left him wept over his loss. "I sent her two dozen roses. She refused them, saying, 'Last year a single rose might have done. It's too late now.' She smashed the television set one day with a beer bottle, during a game I was watching. I said she was crazy and went to a buddy's house to watch the game." Significantly, he admitted to neglecting his daughter also, while he devoted full attention to his "jock" son and to the boy's progress as a young athlete.

These examples of typical problems in the man-woman relationship are directly related to the miseducation of the American male. They are outcroppings, on the adult level, of the masculine mystique inculcated from birth. Another example is the astonishing level of drug addiction, especially alcoholism, among males. In adolescence, drinking is seen as a sign of manliness. One of the rites of initiation into the cult of the big-boys peer group when I was growing up was the ability to chugalug a pint or so of hard liquor. It is but a short step from that to thinking of going on a binge as a sign of masculinity. Many movies have shown us our mythic John Wayne or Charles Bronson heroes resorting to such behavior in response to an emotional crisis.

Because drinking hard liquor is touted as masculine, many men in our society promptly run for the bottle when they feel their adequacy threatened. They prefer it as a

form of escape from women who demand that they meet
them on a more adult ground. Drinking is also one of the
symptoms of low self-esteem, an escape hatch from the
pain of the notion that they are not lovable. Because of its
effects, alcohol abuse leads to antisocial and unlovable
behavior, so it serves to reinforce the conviction of
unlovability. In Minnesota, which has some of the most
advanced drug dependency centers in the country, one
therapy recommended for alcoholic men is group therapy
for the couple as well as individual couple counseling, for
here again the alcohol problem is often seen as symptomatic of the crisis in the man-woman relationship.

"What does woman want?" Freud plaintively asked, and
left us without the hint of an answer, having his own
problems with women. It is a question on the minds of
many men today. Surely everyone knows what women do
not want: They do not want to be considered as receptacles for male sperm; they do not want to be servants to
men; they do not want less pay for the same work that
some man is doing; they do not want discrimination in job
promotions; they do not want. . . . But what *do* they
want? More specifically, what do they want from the men
or the man in their life? Perhaps as a man I am being
terribly presumptuous in even offering the question to
myself. And surely I risk being more than presumptuous
when I essay some possible responses to the question. Yet I
sally forth like Don Quixote because I'm afraid we've had
all too many explorations of what's wrong in the man-
woman relationship, where the problems originate, and
how dreadful things are, with too few people offering even
a hint of positive steps that might be taken to turn this

crisis into a moment of true growth in understanding between men and women.

What does a woman want from her husband? Well, in the sixties and early seventies many women made the mistake of thinking that their path to liberation lay in freeing themselves from their husbands. They thought that was what they wanted. That thought was fostered by the anti-masculine pronouncements abounding in the early literature of the women's movement. Today some of those women readily admit they made a mistake. They found they were freed from the sense of being very important to someone else. Some were freed to cry from loneliness instead of from frustration. As one woman said, "Nobody told me how often I'd cry myself to sleep after the divorce —more often than I ever did before." Some found it freed them to raise their children alone—a 24-hour-a-day, 7-day-a-week unshared and, for many, financially unaided, responsibility. As someone once said, "The grass is always greener on the other side of the fence until you get over there and discover it's astroturf."

So I don't think many women really want out of their relationships with their husbands. What they really want, if I hear them at all correctly, is that their men grow up. Single or married, the articulate, self-possessed, self-supporting woman finds herself too often confronting the tender ego of the male who wants a woman who will look up to him (which implies his elevated status and her genuflection at his shrine), and who will be, or appear to be, dependent upon him in those ways (emotionally or financially or intellectually) that will make him feel strong. If she doesn't play this game, he may feel uncomfortable with her, threatened by her, ill at ease in her company. Or, as

mentioned earlier, he may want her to meet all his needs—
emotional, physical, nurturing, supportive—as his mother
did, without his paying much attention to any of her needs.
In either case, then, what she wants of the man in her life is
that he be a grown-up person.

But what do we mean by grown-up? We touched upon
this at the conclusion of the first chapter. If the men of our
time are to live up to the women of our time, then I think
that they must take a long, hard look at their upbringing
and their assumptions as men. How much of my life is lived
as a role I am playing, trying to "be a man" in the eyes of
other men rather than having the courage to be myself?
Consider for a moment a simple, tiny example of this sort
of thing. One of my favorite before-dinner drinks is a sweet
vermouth with a twist of lemon. Yet, on more than one
occasion when ordering this, I've had men who were ordering a scotch or "double martini, very dry" exclaim, "Why
don't you have a man's drink?" I've often wondered how
many men really would have preferred a daiquiri, or even a
soft drink, but were afraid of losing esteem as "real men"
for ordering less than hard liquor. The TV commercial of
the macho athlete ordering "Schlitz light" is an attempt to
overcome the notion that ordering light beer is somehow
unmanly. Sometimes the assertion of oneself takes such
simple forms as rejecting pressures of that sort.

The courage to be myself and not play roles implies, of
course, the courage to examine myself and find out who I
am. If the criteria for manliness are uncertain in our time, it
is because too few men have had the courage to reexamine
the attitudes inculcated in them in their early years and to
question the validity of such conditioning today. While
many men are ready to pay lip service to the notion of

women's equality as persons, even to agree on the important aspects of man-woman relationships, men continue to
lag behind women in doing the hard work of digging into
themselves and seeing what historical baggage they can
jettison, what chains from the past they can saw off, to
bring themselves greater emotional freedom.

That introspective look into ourselves to confront what
we consider masculinity to be for us is the first task for any
man who wishes to begin the process of growth. It is a
process that can be continued by reading, among other
books, the symposium *Men and Masculinity*, edited by
Joseph Pleck and Jack Sawyer,[3] and Warren Farrell's *The
Liberated Man*.[4] Such books can help any man confront in
himself the questions he must raise if he is to even begin to
sort out his conditioned responses from his authentic feelings about himself and his relationships with women.

Sören Kierkegaard was only echoing the ancient proverb
"Know thyself" and Shakespeare's "To thine own self be
true" when he urged his readers to "be that self which one
truly is." If many men today are leading inauthentic lives it
is because they have not taken the time to find out who
they are.

＊   Freud left the popular impression that we are unfree
creatures, victims of our unconscious drives and instincts.
Marx claimed we were economically determined creatures,
victims of the system. Darwin argued, as did Spencer, that
we were biologically determined. Too many of us men
today seem to have accepted this status of victimhood; but
we do this at our own peril. The fact is that we are
responsible creatures, free to choose our own course. No
one need remain a victim of his or her upbringing or of
unexamined assumptions. We really can open ourselves up

to the questioning that leads to growth. Doing some of the
indicated reading is a first step in that direction. Furthermore, we men might begin to pay attention to what the
women in our lives are trying to tell us. Even though some
of the strongest male chauvinists are women, still many
mature women are challenging their men to grow beyond
the stereotype, to permit themselves a greater emotional
latitude, to grow more fully human.

I personally do not hear my female clients telling their
husbands to define themselves only in terms of wifely
needs or to dedicate their lives simply to serving their
wives' desires. I do hear them calling for us to have the
courage to drop our masks and our role-playing and to
begin to search for new and more authentic ways of treating ourselves and of relating to them.

Perhaps most crucial to our growth as men is that we
learn to take the risks of disclosing ourselves to those we
love. For there can be no authentic loving that does not
involve self-revelation. It is only in authentic love relationships—ones in which we are openly listening to one
another, in which we are touching one another on ever-
deepening levels of personal awareness—that we begin to
gain a sense of personal fulfillment. As we will be pointing
out later in this book, men who seek that sense of personal
fulfillment in a job, in material possessions, in medals or
goals, find those accomplishments inadequate substitutes
for the sense of loving and being loved by another.[5]

Likewise it is here—as an expression of that intimacy,
that self-revelation, that caring for another—that sexual
freedom has its foundation. By sexual freedom I mean not
promiscuity but the freedom to spontaneously, creatively
be myself with the beloved and to give myself away in

joyful surrender without fear of reproach or hurt. For it is not in technologizing their sexuality that men will find the joy of sexual release, but in deepening their appreciation of sexual union as a deeply human personal encounter.

Having the strength to step back and question one's own role-playing is a sign of mature manliness. The rigid man is not showing manly strength but the rigor mortis of one already dead but not yet buried. The living man has the strength to stay open to growth, to take new risks with himself to put life on a more honest and open footing. That openness and honesty with ourselves is the first step toward openness and honesty with others. But whereas the macho male might brutalize others, walk on their feelings, cause them great pain and say that he is "only being frank" (which is usually preceded by the word "brutally," as in "I'm going to be brutally frank with you"), the real man has the consideration to express his conviction, his opinion, or his judgment with honesty but without insulting the other or trampling on the other's feelings. That "brutally frank" approach smacks of the competitive trip, of crushing one's opponent in order to feel one's own strength. A man assured of himself doesn't need such exercise of his power to hurt in order to feel strong. He can be gentle precisely because he knows his own strength. Which leads to the next hallmark of the man, the gentleman: He does respect and reverence other persons.

Women who complain of the men in their lives as "not caring for my feelings, not listening, always walking all over me, talking down, treating me like a child, not giving a damn about me" are describing a male victim of the masculine mystique. If we have heard those remarks directed at us, we ought to examine ourselves carefully for the cause.

Usually, in my own case, the cause was the same: a lack of respect for the woman's personhood. The comment was a warning signal that I was not living up to my own ideals. The mature man, in touch with his own personhood, has the ground for appreciating and reverencing the personhood of others. The basic sign of this lack of respect is not paying attention to the other. Paying attention is a profound sign of love for another. My attentiveness to you tells you that you are important to me. The fact that I am truly listening to you, not interrupting or discounting what you say, but seeking to hear it, to empathize with it, tells you that you are as important to me as my own self—perhaps even more important, for I've laid down my preoccupations in order to let your thoughts, your feelings, enter into me.

One of the hallmarks I've found stamped on all the real men I've ever met has been that of openness to laughter. Not the cynical laughter of the sadist enjoying another's defeat, but laughter at one's own foibles, the willingness to take oneself lightly when that is in order, and the ability to laugh with a real sense of humor at the absurdities we all too often experience. This sort of laughter is the open gateway to enjoyment. The ability to enjoy, to rejoice in life, is greatly increased when one can laugh at oneself, for there the material for laughter is always at hand.

Manliness, the sort of manliness that may enable men to cope more effectively with the man-woman crisis in our times, is not a set of trophies to be won and put on a shelf. There is no classroom in which it can be learned. Most men and women today find manliness difficult to define, for many of the qualities found admirable in men are equally admirable in women. Yet I do think that the beginning of a definition of masculinity can be found in those men who listen to their own feelings and to those of the women in their lives. In both sets of feelings we have sources of insight into what we might do to rid ourselves of the oppression of the male-female stereotypes that are so often the source of conflict between men and women today.

I opened this chapter speaking of the shattering impact of this century on the functional roles of men and women. No longer does the tribe or nation determine by tradition or taboo what form our relationships must take. Today men face the task of creating for themselves the form, style, and quality of their lives and their relationships. That work of re-creating themselves and their relationships with women is a deeply personal task. Each of us is an absolutely unique person. We each have had our own experiences of what it is to grow up male. We each have our own history, our own fears. Yet it is a mistake to think that we are and must remain victims of our history. Indeed, the risk, the challenge, the effort of re-creating ourselves is one of the highest labors of love any man can undertake.

> It is one of life's miracles that every organism has a unique combination of genes which is not apt to recur even in a population of quadrillions. . . . More obvious even than genetic diversity is the uniqueness of each individual's response to his particular environment . . . the human personality is man's prime creation.[6]

The more we move away from stereotypical roles and responses, the more we express our uniqueness. We have little to do with our genetic uniqueness, but we have everything to do with our free responses to that challenge of our environment and the calls for growth from those we love. To respond affirmatively to the call for growth is to take the first step toward appreciating ourselves more fully, enjoying our life more abundantly, and turning the crisis of the man-woman relationship in our time from a crisis leading to divorce between the sexes into a crisis leading to real growth in unity for both of us.

Reflection/Discussion Questions

1. What evidence do you see around you of the man-woman crisis?

2. What evidence do you see, in your community, of alcohol operating in the male mystique?

3. Do you think that what women want from life now is different from what they wanted in earlier decades?

4. How capable are you—and others—of changing your views of masculinity?

5. (For men:) How recently did the significant woman in your life say to you, "You don't listen"? What was your response?

6. Have televised sports been a source of conflict in your marriage? If so, how do you respond?

Notes

1. *Des Moines Register*, April 11, 1977.

2.   Quoted in Vance Packard, *The Sexual Wilderness: The Contemporary Upheaval in Male-Female Relationships* (New York: David McKay, 1968), p. 274. Mr. Packard does not give his source for the May quote.

3.   Englewood Cliffs, N.J.: Prentice-Hall, Spectrum Books, 1974.

4.   New York: Bantam Books, Inc., 1975.

5.   See *The Art of Loving*, a series of cassette tapes by Clayton C. Barbeau (Cincinnati: St. Anthony Messenger Tapes, 1976).

6.   Saul Rosenzweig, "Sexual Autonomy as an Evolutionary Attainment, Anticipating Proceptive Sex Choice and Idiodynamic Bisexuality," in *Contemporary Sexual Behavior: Critical Issues in the 1970's*, ed. Joseph Zubin and John Money (Baltimore and London: Johns Hopkins University Press, 1973), p. 217.

Chapter 3

Corporate Castration

In the last chapter I indicated some of the ways in which the male mystique, when confronted with the challenge of grown-up women, has led to a crisis in man-woman relationships. I have seen many marriages suffering pain, dislocation, and upset because of that crisis rooted in the male's fear that if he truly expresses himself he will be less "masculine" in his wife's eyes. Yet all she wants is that he be less "masculine" in that stereotyped image and more fully the man she knows him to be capable of being, a person able to reveal himself in intimacy to her, to share on the levels of humanity she considers most fundamental. But if what women want offers a good clue for us regarding personal exploration and growth, it is useful to raise the corresponding question: What do men want?

I doubt that many males have taken sufficient time to reflect upon what they want. A minor social revolution, perhaps a major one, would occur if more males were to pose that question to themselves. Surely our response to that question helps us see our priorities.

I can speak only for myself in responding to that question. I want to grow in my ability to express the love within me and to receive the love offered to me. I want to continue in that process, which I have already enjoyed, of having my life become ever richer as I discover myself through those moments of being touched by and touching another human being on the varied levels of human experience. I want to continue growing ever more alive by getting in touch not only with my own pains and joys but with the pains and joys of those who share their lives with me: my family, my friends of both sexes, my clients, yes, even the most casual acquaintance made on bus or plane as I pilgrim through life. I want to rid myself as much as possible of the fear of disclosing myself, which I think is the major barrier to loving, for I see it as based upon my fear and suspicion of the other (he or she might hurt me). I see that fear as a stumbling block to my living a more exuberantly loving life. Yes, I want to be known by you and to know you on something other than the superficial levels of our uniforms, our roles, our positions. I want to feel valued for who I am in myself and not for what I accomplish, not for my title, not for my income—not for any of those accidentals, but for my substance: me. I want to experience an increase in the freedom that I already know is open to me, what the New Testament calls "the freedom of the sons of God." I am well aware that freedom is not an end in itself, not merely freedom *from* something, but a freedom *for* something. I want that increase in freedom (which is nurtured through my risking love and being loved) so that I can more authentically reveal myself. I want to be open to new experiences of the love that feeds our exuberance, that alone makes for a life lived in joy, a life worth living, a life authentically lived. I don't want the stale, unprofitable kind of life in which all too many seem to imprison themselves, and which I have tasted. I want to live as a human being whose being is truly human, and I want to die having lived well.

In saying that, I don't think I express wants that are foreign to any man or any woman, for they seem the common desires of all persons. Unfortunately, all too many seem not to have asked themselves what they truly want. And all too many men have been conditioned out of expressiveness, educated away from getting in touch with their own needs and wants. They are conditioned to play the game of the male mystique, and that conditioning is often reinforced by their work situation. Many men work in an environment hostile to the "wants" just mentioned. Their job demands that they limit their opportunities to grow into the men they might become. Those conditions and the attitudes behind them put up strong supportive props to the masculine role. And by choosing to stay in that masculine role, males often lose their freedom to be men. The masculine mystique as it applies to much of the contemporary work scene is therefore a castrating mystique.

Even two generations ago, there were still areas of human endeavor where raw aggressiveness, toughness, and brute assertiveness were very much needed. Raw physical strength was vital for many jobs, whether that of the stevedore hand-loading cargo or the farmer using his mules to pull boulders from the field. For all our put-downs of the macho types, they did, after all, explore the new lands, settle this continent, build the railroads, found the industries, and break their backs in those industries. And because the land needed such men—men as ready to kill as to die, men as cold as the winter snows they fought, as hard as the steel they were hammering out—we developed the "he-man" breed and gave birth to the mystique. My father recalled arriving as a boy at a railroad station in the West where a fresh corpse swung from the station porch. A purse snatcher had just received the rough and ready justice of the time as a courtesy to the victimized lady.

In those days men set themselves tasks that took great initiative, courage, risk of failure, and mighty hard work— whether it was creating a farm out of the wilderness, plunging a hole into a mountainside in search of gold as my wife's great-grandfather did, or building a logging mill in the North as her grandfather did. These tasks, when successfully accomplished, could be seen as the fruit of their manly labor.

In the past such work, and even survival itself, depended upon cultivating many of the qualities we refer to as part of the male mystique. And that mystique was balanced at the time by an equally clear definition of the feminine role. Women, while expected to be able to endure rugged hardships as well as the men did, were not expected to perform the same functions. If the man's task was to wrest from the earth whatever would put bread on the table, to fight off the wolves or the human predators, the woman's was to tend the hearth, put up the preserves for winter, make and mend the clothes, cook the meals, and bear the children who, if male, would be expected to do a man's work at age ten or twelve. In short, the maintenance and survival chores demanded and got a clear demarcation of roles and functions. The rugged individualism that was preached had its basis in the fact that the society at large did little to aid the individual who fell on hard times. The Social Darwinism that was still much in evidence into the late Thirties maintained that it was the strongest, the fittest, who survived and prospered economically. The weak fell by the wayside, and this was seen as the inevitable order of things. The man who imported Spencer—the major proponent of Social Darwinism—into this country to advance his own theories was Andrew Carnegie, whose own rise to fortune, like Rockefeller's, was based upon ruthless competition that drove more than one competitor not only out of business but into suicide. There was ready ground in America for such a theory as the economic survival of the fittest individual, for our Puritanism taught that the person predestined for heaven was obviously going to be blessed by God while on earth. Thus arose our phrase "a no-good" to denote the man who had failed to pile up material goods —a moral judgment based upon an economic fact.

Out of such ground—historical, philosophical, theological—does the male mystique spring. Yet we don't have to look far to see that times have changed. Just as we no longer swing purse snatchers from the nearest lamppost as a gallant act of homage to assuage the wounded feelings of the lady, neither do we today have many occupations open to men that require them to test their physical toughness to the very limits. Few jobs demand an aggressive, competitive spirit whereby the individual can gain great personal satisfaction at producing something as the hallmark of his achievement, be it a prospering farm, a producing gold mine, a sawmill, an oil or steel empire. Feeding the computer in the bureaucracy on the governmental levels or

doing paper work on the corporate levels has become the
mainstay of life for most. Even the male stevedore uses a
forklift, and while he might take some pride in operating it
well, the job is no longer restricted to men. A "ditchdig-
ger" is today more often than not a machine, as is an
"earth-mover." The "men at work" sign over the last
manhole I saw was repainted to read "persons at work" and
the last telephone "repairman" I saw climbing a pole was a
woman. One wonders how much of the initial resistance to
opening such jobs to women came from the fact that the
"male mystique" had classified such jobs as testimonies to
manliness. If these jobs no longer proved one was a man,
where was one to prove it?

More important, however, is the fact that we have
moved in the last generation or two from a society of
producers to a society of consumers. The products con-
sumed are often produced by a small minority of workers.
Today some factories are almost totally automated, and the
managerial, sales, promotion, clerical, and data-processing
staffs vastly outnumber the factory workers. In the bank-
ing, investment, and insurance businesses, nothing visible is
produced; a money flow is recorded and processed through
computers and telex machines. At nearly all levels of such
office work there is little room for individual initiative,
rugged individualism, or a sense of personal achievement.
The work flow is generally so parceled out that the individual handles one portion, one aspect, of the overall task of a
firm. The male finds himself with no choice but to be a
passive instrument in carrying out corporate policy, which
often enough involves compromising his integrity in many
little, if not large, ways. At the same time he may find
himself involved in promoting such frivolous ideas as the

superiority of one hair shampoo over another, neither of which he uses.

We have moved from the time when a worker needed certain specific skills to do something by hand, through a period when he had to operate a machine to do it, to the present when he finds the machine operating itself. We are not only eliminating many of our semi-skilled workers; many of our non-professional "skilled" workers of only ten or twenty years ago are no longer needed. One sociologist who studied the employment situation of persons in the top five-percent income bracket in the United States found that in 1950, 42% of this leadership group was self-employed; in 1960, it was only 26%. In that same decade, among the same group, salaried positions rose from only 28% to 48%. For the last thirty years we have seen a consistent falloff in the number of persons successfully running their own small business, and a corresponding increase among the managerial group in corporations. In the past generation we have not only seen the move from self-employment to salaried employment but have witnessed corporations, through constant mergers, growing larger than ever; small corporations are being swallowed up by the larger ones. More and more persons are working for fewer and fewer conglomerates. And within the conglomerates, power is in the hands of a very few. In at least one situation of which I am personally aware, one man at the head of a conglomerate has to initial every contract from every one of the literally dozens of subsidiaries, which include not only book publishing houses but gift shops, audiovisual companies, correspondence schools, and other businesses.

The impact of all this on the American man is often overlooked. On the personal level he experiences a direct conflict. He has been raised in the older and still-taught ideals of rugged individualism, self-direction, personal integrity, and aggressive pursuit of personal achievement. But he confronts a large, hierarchically organized work structure that requires his compliance and conformity on the lower levels. If he rises to higher levels in the firm through showing his loyalty in this way, he becomes a tool of corporate policy and must successfully manipulate others toward reaching the corporate goals. Either way he is a prisoner.

If a man chooses to fit into this corporate structure, he must be a striver within that organization, behaving according to whatever mode is required to "get ahead" in the hierarchy. In short, to prove himself "a man," an effectively functioning male in our society (at least on the job), he must set aside the very qualities of independence and aggressiveness that his upbringing told him were most male, or at least he must channel them into modes of behavior fitting the situation. Thus, some firms set up competitions among their salesmen, carrying the playing-field ethic of winning teams onto the sales boards. But there is a more subtle competition going on at the same time. Since few rise to the top in any firm of any size, a man turns his competitive spirit into beating his peers to the promotion, looking good to his superiors, obtaining status symbols. One attorney for a major corporation pointed to a rug on the floor of his office and the two bookcases along the wall and said, "That rug and that second book-case mean nothing to you, but they mean a helluva lot to nine out of ten persons on this floor."

Inevitably in such a setting, the man does receive reinforcement for one aspect of the male mystique: He must not show sensitivity, vulnerability. Were he to do this before his subordinates, they might see it as a weakness, and his authority thereby would be undermined. If he demonstrates such vulnerability or sensitivity to his peers, they could use it to beat him out of a promotion. And he surely cannot let any weakness show before his superiors or he would not be considered leadership material. Job promotion itself becomes a goal. Fasteau quotes a young executive as saying:

> "You never stand still. You're either moving ahead or moving downstairs. And once they catch you standing still, you're on your way down." The aggressive, motivated individual is a generalist and will do any job. The way a person gets to the top, very simply, is to take two- and three-year stints, two years here, two years there. He's capable of moving. They like his ability to continually uproot his family. Is he willing to go out to Seattle, Washington? . . . it proves that he is interested in going to the top.[1]

Vance Packard's *A Nation of Strangers* is devoted to depicting this nomadic existence, these company gypsies, and the accompanying fragmentation of the family, the loss of a sense of community, and the effects of rootlessness on the psyche. Packard points out that three-fourths of those moved by long-distance hauling companies work at the managerial, professional, and technical level of large corporations or government agencies.

The wife of one corporate employee, upon reading this, wrote me:

I think it unfair to place total blame for this upon the male. There is also the female who plays a role as "Corporate Wife." How many of the women complaining about their husbands are actually willing to forgo the status and the possessions their husbands earn by such behavior?

When George worked for one of the large accounting firms, any evaluation for promotion contained information on what I was doing—was it the proper sort of volunteer work and clubs conducive to our meeting people who would be prospective clients?

When he made Supervisor, I was invited to a posh luncheon where, along with other wives, we heard the wife of one of the top executives speak on the role the wife played in furthering her husband's career. This woman's account included the many cultural and civic accomplishments she carried out from her Bel Air mansion. Bleah!

I observed these women in action at the local country club with their golf, tennis, and bridge groups; the competitiveness and power plays that took place were not at all unlike those going on in the office. Having spent some years as member of our local country club and tennis club, I found many of the men to be more authentic and real than their ambitious wives.[2]

The retired vice-president of a major U.S. corporation, speaking of his wife's present bitterness at what she termed her "years of neglect" by him and the "single parenting" she'd had to do as he rose to the rarified heights of corporate power, said, "But, damn it, she was the one who constantly pushed and shoved and urged me to be more ambitious. Now she punishes me for having paid the price of getting to the top."

The struggle to the top can be fierce and dirty. A friend of mine was considered a first-rate trouble-shooter for his firm. He was tough and capable of going into a branch that was not performing well and shaping up the operation. He always increased the company's revenues, in some instances doubling the revenues of a branch he had reorganized. There came the day when the head office wanted him to uproot his family and move to another city. He thought the matter over and decided that his family's needs were best met where they were, that the move wasn't necessary anyway. He told me before the meeting at which he was to announce this decision that he would be fired. I expressed disbelief, given his record of accomplishment for the firm. He responded: "That doesn't matter. My putting my family first means I'm not a company man." That afternoon he was fired—an object lesson for those who place personal integrity, true morality, and human values above the supposed needs of the corporation. But it had a further lesson in it, for he learned during the meeting who had instigated the request for his transfer. It was another executive in his office, one rung higher on the ladder. Threatened by his subordinate's good performance and knowing he would not accept a transfer, this achiever used the "transfer" to remove a potential threat to his own position.

Work is a crucial activity for any of us. Albert Camus once commented, "Without work, all life goes rotten. But when work is soulless, life stifles and dies." By my own definition, however, true work is creative work, an

endeavor that taps our human resources, that confronts us
with a challenge to grow, that provides us an opportunity
to actualize our potentialities for producing something that
elicits pride. This I would call work with a soul. It is
meaningful activity, a task or set of tasks that has meaning
and that helps bring us a sense of personal satisfaction. It is
also one of the ways in which men have found an authentic
expression of their personalities.

Unfortunately, we have less and less such work available
for either men or women. We seem instead to have jobs,
which we do to pay the bills. When the only meaning of
the job is to earn money to pay the bills, then the job can
be wearing and debilitating. Even so, for many men the
job is the means chosen to prove their manliness. They
strive to do this by increasing the amount of money they
make or by elevating their status in the corporate structure.
Here we have the situation where work is not a creative task
in which something of value is produced for society as a
whole but is simply a tool whereby the man seeks to prove
something to himself in competition with—perhaps at the
expense of—others within the firm.

Apparently there is no limit to what some males will put
up with to prove themselves this way. Some will sacrifice
themselves and their families on the altar of that god. I was
at a large meeting of the executives of an international
organization last year, the guest of one of the executives.
With some pride my host told me about one man I was
about to meet. "He's the best hatchet man we've got," he
said, "absolutely ruthless. Yet he does it with a smile. He
can fire a man who's been with us twenty-five years and not
twitch a muscle and have the guy think he's done him a
favor."

Here is where the cult of toughness at the top echelons comes into play. But it is also at work in those corporations that test their young execs by transferring them from one hellhole to another to see if they can take it before moving them to a more comfortable regional or head office. To cite Fasteau again:

The cult of toughness can also be seen in the initiation rites of the professions and some businesses. Pledgees are typically put through the ordeal of working incredibly long hours, a proof of the ability to "take it." Hospital interns are worked around the clock. Architecture students, Caroline Bird points out, are given design problems that can't be completed by the time they are due unless the team works through the night. Law firms, especially the big ones which can afford it [and both Fasteau and his wife are attorneys], are legendary for giving young associates impossible, and often phony, deadlines and for making them draft long complicated documents from scratch "for the experience" instead of using others as models.[3]

And the young executive he quoted earlier reported, "All first presentations or reports by new managers are ripped to shreds regardless of their actual quality."[4]

Such initiation rites of course insure that those willing to put up with them will do the corporate bidding, however stupid it may seem. It also helps create the desire to perpetuate the system: "I went through hell; so will you."

But when does the struggle for status in the corporate hierarchy end? From all the evidence in the articles and sociological interviews and psychological studies I've read, it apparently doesn't—for most. Is that surprising? In a consumer society where the aim of the job is to win enough money to buy the goods that will prove success, when does one have enough? In a system where only a few ever rise to the top, isn't there always somebody who has more? Perhaps the most frustrating part of the work structure for the American male is that the cost of "proving himself" on the job is that he sacrifice his feelings, submerge his own desires, forgo the satisfactions of fulfilling and creative labor, and be constantly on guard against subordinates and peers while appearing, in the eyes of his superiors, to be totally in control.

For many it is quite depersonalizing and hence "de-manning." Thus many of those who comply with the demands of their corporate labors during the day seek release in their private lives. We find the hyper-eroticism evidenced by the "swinging singles scene"; the hedonistic and infantile pursuits that abound in our major cities are basically supported as recreation by young executives and middle-echelon personnel. All these are attempts to fill the vacuum left by the loss of freedom and creativity on the job as well as to alleviate the tensions generated by the daily labor of rigidly conforming to such corporate standards. The emphasis upon "scoring" sexually appears in this context as an attempt to reaffirm one's manhood after the depersonalizing and thus castrating effects of one's daily labors.

I do not mean to imply that this castration is occurring only in the world of corporations. The academic world, the world of medicine and law, journalism, publishing, and the media are all emulating these procedures. It is the American way of business. About ten years ago a man, unhappy in his position in Washington, put an ad in the

New York Times Sunday edition: "Well-educated professional man seeks change of occupation. Wants creative,
stimulating and socially worthwhile work. Will consider
any offers. Salary a secondary consideration." He let the ad
run for one week beyond the Sunday, so he reached literally
millions of readers. He got three replies. Two were from
insurance companies offering him a job as a salesman; one
was from a writer researching an article on the death of
rugged individualism in the U.S. who wanted to know
what response my friend had gotten from his ad.

Each of us has his or her own sources of personal
anxiety. The sense of anomie, depression, feelings of frustration, or other emotional states any of us may experience
are rooted in our own past, present, or anticipated situation.
But I believe that one of the great sources of those discom-
forts and dislocations of self that many men share is the
conditions under which they work. The fact that their
major expenditure of energy is basically lacking in true
human meaning contributes to their dis-ease. Their work
does not often give them a sense of a job well done.
Spending days full of competition without victory and
replete with demands to be "tough" but with no room to
permit being a real man, i.e., to show one's integrity or
personhood, leads to a sense of being unmanned in the
very area where accomplishment used to help one feel
manly: work. Feelings of depression, insecurity, and even
inadequacy result.

This situation also leads many to a sort of futurism.
Happiness or a sense of satisfaction will come when I get a
raise or a promotion or make that move to New York.
Tomorrow I will be able to live authentically. Such males
postpone living and yet resent having to do so. No wonder

I meet so much anger in my dealings with men from the business community. They are angry with themselves and with their world. That is the anger that often produces our suicides and our heart attacks.

But sometimes I have seen that anger produce a crisis, a depression or illness that causes a man to pause and reflect. Then a man may change his life-style. He may move toward breaking the chains that hold him. He finally takes a long, hard look at his priorities in life and reevaluates his life's work. Such men, at last, have asked themselves, "What do I really want out of life?"

The unconscious is very often ahead of the conscious in alerting us to this question. Thus, one thirty-five-year-old middle-management executive sought counseling for what he called his "depression." He was constantly upset with his wife; they kept having arguments that he admittedly provoked. He took scant pleasure in his infant son, formerly a source of pride and delight. Though he was in a field he had trained himself for and could pinpoint no immediate cause of irritation there, he was dissatisfied with his work, could barely drag himself from bed to get to the office. He was beginning to drink more heavily and had returned to a smoking habit he had dropped some five years before. He felt some ambivalence about the fact that his wife made more money than he did, but he denied this as a major source of irritation, pointing out that their combined incomes were "necessary" to sustain their life-style.

I asked him: "What do you want out of life?"

He looked bewildered. "I don't know. Just what everybody wants, I suppose."

"And what do you suppose everybody wants?"

He was thoughtful, finally responded: "To get ahead, I guess."

I pointed out that he had a lovely home, he and his wife had their own careers, their own cars, their physical health, they had a healthy young son, sufficient income to live a most comfortable life, so what was he "getting ahead" to? What was his goal?

He didn't know.

Pressed, he granted that many were trying to "get ahead" to the same material level as he was, even while he was pushing himself to "get ahead" to some as-yet-undefined goal of increased wealth or status. As our sessions progressed, he discerned that his dissatisfaction with his present life—dissatisfaction that he was blaming on his wife, his child, his work—was truly the result of his confronting on a deeper level the emptiness within himself. It was an emptiness that would not, he came to realize, be filled by a larger bank account or a more exalted title. For the first time in his life, he had to ask himself consciously about the purpose of his existence.

Another young executive responded to such an inner confrontation by resigning his position and founding an organization to help troubled youngsters. His management skills, his knowledge of the business world, aided him in enlisting corporate support for the work.

No honest labor need demean us. One meatcutter, whose job is to drop a ham from a carcass with seven whacks of his knife—a job he has been doing for a quarter century—takes pride in his skill. He enjoys the camaraderie of his work crew. They enjoy their beers at lunch together; they often go fishing or hunting together. Asked why he is working, he would respond that he does it to support his

70

family. He might not say it, but supporting his family is his major creative labor. He has only a high-school education himself, but he has put three children through college. He enjoys their love and respect as well as the continued love and companionship of his wife. He knows the purpose, the meaningfulness of his work: It supports this community of life and love.

Too many men, however, suggest that they are working for the family, but they discover that they are sacrificing their family on the altar of their occupations.

One of my dearest friends, stunned by the death of my wife, examined his own work schedule. He owns a travel agency, a three-person office. The phones never stop ringing, and he often worked overtime to serve his clients. "I love my work," he said, "but my wife and I had a talk after Myra's death. I realized I was losing out on valuable time with the family." So he hired another person and put himself and each of his staff on a four-day week with the same salary and benefits as before.

More enlightened corporation heads are becoming sensitive to the need for humanizing their structures. On several occasions the president or vice-president of a major corporation has invited me to hold a seminar for executives and their spouses on coping with stress, familial communications, and similar problems. Surely their motives include understanding that the man or woman with an unhappy home situation is not going to be an effective producer on the job. However, the executives responsible were also, in my experience, concerned for the human persons involved. They did not want to see marriages destroyed by the work. They sought to help families wounded by alcoholism or by the other escape hatches people use to cope with stress.

One such executive told me:
We were a small company at the start. We had
brainstorming sessions that included everybody, and
everybody had their say. People disagreed openly
with me or my partner. A lot of creative energy was
unleashed there, and the company benefited. In fact,
we were swamped with success. Now we have so
many people, I see faces I don't recognize. And now
we have people who are afraid to speak up, each one
wanting to be on the right side—whatever that is—of
a discussion. There's jockeying for position now, in-
fighting. I don't like it. We had a community before.
We don't now. And I think we're going to lose the
creative energy that got us here.
Significantly, on a "Day for Married Couples" sponsored
by one national firm at the regional level, the man who
invited me called about two weeks before the event. "We're
not getting the turnout I expected. Everyone is afraid they
might be involved in some sort of group discussion and
have to get 'personal' with others they work with. If it's
okay with you, I'm putting out a memo reassuring them
that the only dialogues will be between the spouses, and
private. Okay?"
    I told him that was what I had planned. He put out the
memo, and we had a capacity audience.
    Such efforts by corporations are helpful, and they are
numerous, but (as is obvious from the comments of both
the men quoted above) it seems very difficult to maintain a
human atmosphere in the workplace—the sort of atmosphere the meatcutter has among his small crew of co-
workers. Still, the task of seeking to make our place of
work more human and humanizing is not impossible. It

involves accepting individual responsibility for cultivating and maintaining a personal—rather than a competitive—approach to those around one. Corporate bodies are composed of human beings. And corporate bodies that are dehumanizing and depersonalizing can be changed by the persons within them. Whether shipping clerk or vice-president, each man within a corporate structure makes a contribution to the quality of that corporate life. When these men maintain their personhood, show the courage to be themselves and to truly befriend one another in their workplace, they make a real contribution toward having a community of co-workers, a human endeavor, as opposed to a collective of animated tools competing for such trivia as a rug on the floor or a second bookcase or an office with a window. If one is working in a place that does not permit such humanity to flower, then it is time to ask the hard questions: "Who is in charge of my life? What am I living for? How does this job contribute to my sense of self-worth and to the advancement of my growth as a human being?" And then the ultimate questions: "What do I truly want to get out of life? What do I want to give to life? Where can I better achieve these goals? How am I stopping myself from making a change?"

The persons within dehumanizing corporate bodies must either change those bodies or at least refuse to collaborate with them. Either decision is a manly, creative step toward making our workplaces, our society, and our personal lives more human.

Reflection/Discussion Questions

1. Do you see "rugged individualism" as less relevant to our times than it used to be?

2. Does this chapter's discussion of corporate life match your experiences of it?

3. How important is work satisfaction to you?

4. How do you think corporations could be more supportive of the human needs of employees?

5. What do you want out of life?

6. If you did not need the income, would you continue at your present work? If not, what would you do?

Notes
1. Marc Fasteau, *The Male Machine* (New York: McGraw-Hill, 1974), p. 121.

2. New York: Pocket Books, 1974, p. 10.

3. Fasteau, p. 126.

4. Ibid.

Chapter 4

The Failure of Success

The psychiatrist and I were among the principals at a weekend symposium. In the course of his remarks he gave an illustration of what he called "the will to fail." He described a man who, at age twenty-three, had resolved that he would have a wife, four children, two cars, a luxury home, and a minimum income of fifty thousand dollars a year, all by the time he was forty-five years old.

The psychiatrist related that the man not only reached each of these goals but had, in fact, surpassed them on the financial level and done so by age forty-three. In spite of this, the psychiatrist went on, the man began to drink excessively, indulged in irresponsible financial behavior which included reckless gambling, and showed other signs of personality disorder. By the time he reached age forty-five, the man had behaved with such total disregard for himself and others that his wife had divorced him and he was bankrupt. The psychiatrist then said, "Now, that's what I call the will to fail."

I disagree with the doctor's evaluation. I do not see his patient's behavior as an example of the "will to fail" at all. A person with the "will to fail" would never have reached any of his goals. On the contrary, at moments of critical choice, those moments when nerve is tested, he would have pulled back, responded in a fashion that kept success out of reach. The person the psychiatrist described did not do this; he did not fail to achieve his goals. He succeeded, and quite admirably. Having set his will on certain achievements, he turned them into realities. He won through to victory on each of his money and status goals. Further, he accomplished the task two years ahead of schedule. He was a resounding success!

His behavior after he stood at the pinnacle of financial success signaled not at all the "will to fail" but a syndrome I've chosen to call "the failure of success." He had succeeded, but success had failed him.

I claim no credit for the title of this chapter. Dr. Esther Milner, a social scientist, first published a book by that title in 1959.[1] Referring to the success mystique as the "touchstone fallacy" of our time, she provides an in-depth and powerful commentary on the effects of that mystique upon our entire social and educational structure and on the fabric of personal relationships.

The fallacy is, of course, that occupational status and the acquiring of consumer goods will provide a sense of inner peace, a modicum of happiness not presently enjoyed. Seldom do men spell out their goals as clearly as that psychiatrist's patient did. He knew the very day when he could declare himself a "winner," a "success," in the competitive struggle. When that day came, however, nothing happened. And that is precisely where the American

Dream failed him. Success had not delivered whatever he had assumed it would provide.

What had he expected? Was it what we call happiness? Perhaps he wanted a sense of inner tranquility. Or would "success" put an end to anxious striving and replace it with inner freedom, exaltation, or joy in life?

His clearly defined goals couldn't of themselves supply any of those gifts of the spirit, for they were all material. He viewed even his "wife and four children," specified before he had even met the woman, as acquisitions, possessions like the luxurious home and the two cars. No wonder, then, that after achieving his vision of success and finding that he himself was not experiencing his inner life as one whit changed from the day before, he collapsed. He had run the race, won the gold cup he was certain would be filled with the heady wine of joy, only to discover that it held nothing but an inventory of his possessions. One can understand why he threw all away in a fit of disillusionment.

Most men are not so fortunate as to have reality impinge upon their pursuit of the goddess of success. Not having clearly defined what they mean by "success," as he had, many spend their entire lives running toward a goal always in the distance. Such males believe that their present lack of a sense of personal accomplishment, their pervasive discontent, will be dissolved when they get the next promotion, more money, the new home. Often enough, those who do arrive at a point where they have a surfeit of luxury goods—the new home, car, and title—still feel dissatisfied. When they look about to discover why, they often decide it is because of the one leftover from the days of struggle:

their wife. She too, they may decide, must be traded in for a new model.

In actuality, the majority of men do not experience enough material success to confront the fallacy of staking their emotional and psychological well-being on such externals. Their conviction that their manhood itself is being measured by the yardstick of material "success," their belief that their place in the esteem of family, friends, and society depends upon dedicating themselves to the pursuit of status and power—all these provide fuel for a sometimes compulsive striving.

One thirty-five-year-old man, married, father of two, came to see me at the urgings of his worried wife. A member of a small consulting firm, he took a full briefcase of work home with him each evening and on weekends. After dinner he worked. He arose before dawn to put in another stint before breakfast, usually arrived at work an hour earlier than anyone else, and often left an hour later than the others. On weekends he spent hours at work, sometimes going to the office to find the quiet necessary for the task. His wife was less concerned for herself than for his relationship with his young children, to whom he was a stranger.

There was no room for advancement in the firm. It was owner-managed, and all the rest of the staff had equal rank.

No one else, neither his boss nor his peers, put forth such effort as he; no one spent as much time on the job. What then motivated him? It was the conviction that his personal value, his very self-respect, was grounded on his being not merely as good as but *better* than anyone else in the firm. He felt a constant anxiety that should someone make comparisons he might be found wanting. While his is an exaggerated case, this man merely manifests in a more graphic way the basic male fallacy of measuring one's personal worth in competition with other men rather than by assessing the quality of one's love relationships.

If this man made inordinate and patently absurd demands upon himself, he highlights what many others do in less obvious ways. They isolate themselves from others, including their families, hide their softer feelings, dedicate themselves to unsatisfying work, feel threatened by their peers, and make exhaustive demands upon themselves in terms of time and energy. They do this in the hope that someday they will enjoy the fruits of such efforts. Yet, running on a collision course with this blind striving is our human need for personal warmth, the desire to be liked, even loved, on the basis of who we are and not merely on what we do or what we own.

Often such a man turns to his spouse or his children to provide all the emotional and ego support, the reassurance and personal sense of lovability, that once came from a larger circle of friends, from truly worthwhile work, from a personal sense of creative achievement. That demand placed upon the spouse or children is one of the heavier burdens many of today's families bear.

When that demand comes from a person whose major energies and prime-time involvements are dedicated to just the opposite behavior in the larger world, and from one who is often inarticulate in expressing what he is truly feeling, the stage is set for marital conflict and family tensions. Because so many men are incapable of coping with their deeper feelings and don't know how to handle their intimate relationships at home, we see large numbers of upwardly striving husbands who literally spend less time

with their families—on their days "off"—than they do on
the golf course. On the golf course they can continue the
competitive life, competing against other men or against
their own previous scores. It is a world where they feel
more at home than in the non-competitive world where
love exists.

Of course the inner tensions remain unreleased. Or do
they? I don't think it's at all surprising that we find our
epoch increasingly violent. I speak not only in terms of the
violence that is the staple of our sports and television and
movies, but the random violence endemic to our society
and the domestic violence that accounts for the large
majority of our homicides. One wife of a middle-management executive told me that when she told him that if she
did not receive more truly intimate sharing with him, she
would be driven to seeking it elsewhere or through divorce,
he replied that he would kill her if she tried either—but he
made no offer of increased intimacy. As might be
expected, he also refused to come for marital therapy,
saying "It's your problem, not mine."

Anxiety over success, feelings of inadequacy or helpless-
ness, fear or guilt, all the tensions of the struggle, on the
part of those who do not yet (as the saying goes) "have it
made," become a sort of free-floating hostility. When this
hostility is directed toward oneself—internalized—it can
become the sort of self-hatred that leads to alcoholism or
suicide. Externalized, it finds its easiest targets in wife and
children—and both wife-beating and child-beating are
large-scale problems in our time—or it finds its outlet in
racial prejudice or in the enjoyment of violence vicariously
participated in, as in sports or the television crime show.
That violent kind of hostility is one of the personal

responses to the failure of the success mystique to deliver on its promise. I have the wayward thought that it is the sort of free-floating anger that accounts for the fact that on two occasions in recent months, in separate parts of the country, a commuter, upon being rear-ended in a traffic jam, got out and blew the offender's brains out.

I suggest that the same success mystique accounts for the enormous numbers of men in our business and professional community who are drug-dependent, especially alcohol-dependent. That is one way of seeking escape from tension.

Lately, more persons have begun to recognize, at least theoretically, the fallacy of the success mystique. Even politicians have begun to talk about "lowered expectations," to question the time-hallowed notion that "bigger is better"—in cars or in cities. When even politicians talk that way, we know that such ideas are gaining general acceptance, for politicians always have one finger in the air to test the prevailing winds of public opinion.

There are yet other signs of dissatisfaction with the success mystique. Among the young—and also among some groups of older persons—we have seen the rising popularity of various coercive cults that ask their members to drop out of the anxiety-producing rush for success and give over their liberty of conscience to some charismatic leader. Such ascetic millionaires preach a gospel of detachment in exchange for the security of belonging to a "loving community." Others, and in significant numbers, are turning their backs upon material pursuits and devoting themselves to fundamentalist Christian cults and prayer groups. I think that these, too, are signs of the times, indications that more and more people are aware of the failure of "success" to deliver on its promise of happiness and inner peace.

As a marriage and family therapist specializing in individual and couple counseling, I find similar signs of the times written in personal histories rather than on the level of social or religious movements. I am not alone in finding that if about half my clients are seeking help with problems relating to marriage, the other half are seeking help in re-ordering their priorities, checking out their goals, looking for a more fulfilling life-style.

Not long ago, a gentleman of my acquaintance, a nuclear physicist, left his prestigious and high-paying job in the military establishment, took a cut in pay and prestige, and put his talents to use in a hospital's radiation therapy unit. In his view, the cut in pay and status is more than compensated for by the enormous increase in his sense of doing humanitarian work with his talents rather than sharing responsibility for creating more nuclear terror. This seems a minimal move: to refuse to collaborate in a work that hurts or exploits others.

A few years back, the most talented executive at General Motors, a vice-president who everyone said was in line for the presidency of our largest corporation, resigned in order to devote himself to working with volunteer groups and, if memory recalls his statement, "to do something more worthwhile with my life than make cars and money." When that event was reported on the financial pages of the newspapers across the country, a cynical friend said: "Well, he can afford to do that what with his fortune and his stock in the company." My rejoinder to that was that if the step was so obvious and so easy, why don't we see more millionaire executives of major companies doing likewise?

Some of us do the work we do because we have no options. More of us just don't take the time to explore whether we can find more satisfying ways of dealing with our work or else simply find a type of work at which we would be happier.

It is obvious that success, defined in terms of money and status and consumer goods, does not equate with happiness. But make that statement sometime and note the responses. A typical one is "Well, money may not make you happy, but it sure makes the misery easier to bear." But does it? The names of "successful" entertainment and business and professional persons whose unhappiness ended in suicide are legion. Hemingway was not only the best-known writer in America (his name known even to illiterates who could look at the pictures in *Life*) but one of the best paid. He was also one of the most competitive and most zealous for success, as is testified to by his treatment of F. Scott Fitzgerald and his comment, during his last appearance in Pamplona, that he had "outchekhoved Chekhov." His occupational status or his financial success did not keep him from blowing his head off with a shotgun.

We have too many such examples of the tragic failure of success to fulfill basic human needs. Yet all too many men continue to be all too willing to accept the fallacy that their self-worth and their manliness is measured by that sort of occupational success.

A study made by Jan E. Dizard of the Community and Family Study Center followed 400 marriages from the time of the engagement through 14 to 17 years of marriage.[2] From expressions of mutual happiness and high levels of cooperation and sharing and a marked affection for each other elicited by their first questionnaire, many couples had moved by the time of the final questionnaire to indicating an erosion in their happiness with each other. Half the wives and nearly half the husbands expressed a decline in their happiness together. About sixty percent revealed disagreements that were more frequent and more serious than those in earlier years. Forty percent of the wives and nearly as many of the husbands had considered separation or divorce. For many, demonstrations of affection had diminished. But in an essay based on his study Dizard commented (the emphasis is his):

> Had all of the couples reported declining satisfactions with and commitment to their marriage we could simply say that time takes its toll. No such bromide applies. In fact, what we discovered was that *by and large it was in these couples in which the husband had been most successful in his occupational pursuits that the spouses were most likely to report deterioration* in the marital relationship.[3]

Indeed, the dissatisfaction and the declining levels of happiness for the most successful husbands and their wives were twice as high as that expressed by those couples whose incomes had actually declined—who were, in short, less successful in economic terms. "Success, in other words, doubled the likelihood that the husband and wife's happiness would decline over time."[4] In the same essay Dizard quotes the famous study by Blood and Wolfe[5] of 900 Detroit families that came to the conclusion: "High-income husbands have conspicuously dissatisfied wives."[6]

Not only does the success mystique fail the American male in terms of personal satisfaction; it fails him on the level of his most intimate human contacts: with his wife and children.

Where does that leave us? Obviously, few men can afford to run right out and quit their jobs, even if that appears to be the solution. Nor is it feasible that we all take vows of voluntary poverty. I personally enjoy eggs benedict and champagne for breakfast from time to time. I also know it is nice to be able to pay the mortgage and put food on the family table. But I do think that we men, if we are to live more human and enjoyable lives, need to take a hard look at our personal priorities. To what degree do we set external goals and tell ourselves that happiness will come when we've reached those goals? To what degree are we turning means into ends? To what degree do we put material achievement ahead of human beings, particularly that human being who is ourself? Many men tell themselves that they are working so hard, devoting so much time and energy and effort to getting ahead on the job for the sake of the family, when actually they are sacrificing the family and their own personal enjoyment of their family life for job advancement.

We also need to ask how susceptible we are to the advertising industry whose goal is to create desires in us for things we don't need. It would surely help the economy of many households and ease the burden on many wage earners if they learned to distinguish between wants and needs. The ease with which the majority of us can run right out and purchase on credit what we want makes it easy for us to avoid the question of whether we really *need* the wanted item. Meeting that *want* increases our financial indebtedness and makes it all the more necessary for us to pursue the goddess of financial "success."

Since we earn our wages by spending a certain part of our life-time at the job, it might be helpful for us to look at any product we are considering buying and to translate the money amount into time. How much time did I spend to earn the money I will be spending on this? The answer to that question tells me how much of my life-time I have just paid for this product. Is it worth it? This is one way of sorting out my priorities.

The Judeo-Christian ethic offers us insight into this ordering of our priorities. "What will a man gain by winning the whole world, at the cost of his true self?"[7] "Jesus looked round at his disciples and said to them, 'How hard it will be for the wealthy to enter the kingdom of God!' " It is precisely because financial success so often costs a man his contact with his true self that he does not enter the kingdom of God. When Jesus spoke of the "kingdom of God" as belonging to little children, he was, among other things, reminding us that it is with a child's fresh vision, a child's humility, that we need to look at the gift of our life-time and our enjoyment of that gift. All the possessions in the world will not give us happiness. That kingdom is not out there; it is within ourselves.

Men must ask some hard questions if they are to reassert control over their own lives and begin to experience a fuller life. The first questions are, To what degree do I truly devote my energies to creating myself as a better human being? Does my work help anyone? Does my work help me feel more at home with myself, more at home in the world, more at one with my own family and the entire human family? A further question might well be, To what extent do I live in the future? The pursuit of "success" engages the attention of so many of us precisely because "success" is always just out of our reach.

When I do recognize the need for personal change in some way, what fear do I allow to restrain me? Often in doing therapy I've aided a client to confront his fear openly by having him create a scenario that details, step-by-step, the calamities that might befall him should he do what he says he'd like to do. Often we exaggerate those fearsome possibilities. Just as often, the fear dissolves or is greatly diminished by the time we reach the end of the process. It is the unnamed, the unconfronted fear, the faceless fear, that holds some of us on an occupational path that is corroding our spirit.

Not long ago I had a client who, during his first visit, evidenced obvious fear of something. I asked him about this, and he responded that he was "afraid of failing." I wanted to know what particular failure he feared at that moment. He replied by reminding me that I had told him when the interview was being arranged that I was only agreeing to see him for the first hour. At the end of that initial session, I would decide whether I was the right person to work with him, and he too would decide if I was the right person. Then, if we were both accepting of the other, we'd talk about how many sessions it might take. The fear of failure, the need to be a success at everything, had been drummed into him from earliest youth. He now revealed that he was afraid he wouldn't be a success at becoming a client of mine; he might fail this "interview," and I would refer him elsewhere.

I haven't laughed so hard in a session in many months. And my laughter got him laughing, too, at fear of failure to be accepted as a therapeutic client! I then announced he had come to the right person, that I had never failed in anything. Why, I had done everything perfectly. I had never fallen flat on my face. I had succeeded at everything I had ever tried. I went on extolling my perfection as one grand success until his face showed he thought I was a madman. And then I asked: "If any of that were true, would you want me for a therapist?" He said no. A friend? Again, no. A brother? No.

In point of fact, isn't it true that you and I make our most human contacts, not out of our confrontations from positions of successful achievement, positions of strength, but most surely and most profoundly out of our meeting in our vulnerability, in our moments of sharing in our fears or our tears, our needs, our hurts—yes, our failures? For many men it is only when their dreams of success have failed them that they are able to take the first steps toward a fuller appreciation of life's riches.

Reflection/Discussion Questions

1. Have you tasted the failure of success in your own life?

2. Do you see work life intruding on home life in your community? If so, how?

3. Do you see alternatives to dropping out as a means of relieving the tension in our lives?

4. In what ways, if any, have you lowered your expectations in the last few years?

5. Do you make a habit of distinguishing your wants from your needs?

6. Have you considered that money spent equals lifetime?

Notes

1. *The Failure of Success* (St. Louis, Mo.: Warren J. Green, 1968).

2. *Social Change in the Family* (Chicago: Community and Family Study Center, University of Chicago, 1968).

3. Jan E. Dizard, "The Price of Success," *The Future of the Family*, ed. Louise Kapp Howe (New York: Simon & Schuster, 1972), p. 195.

4. Loc. cit.

5. Robert O. Blood and Donald M. Wolfe, *Husbands and Wives: The Dynamics of Married Living* (New York: Free Press, 1960).

6. Quoted in Dizard, p. 196.

7. Matthew 16:26. This and the other two biblical passages quoted in this paragraph (Mark 10:23 and Luke 18:16-17) are taken from the New English Bible, © The Delegates of the Oxford University Press and The Syndics of the Cambridge University Press, 1961, 1970. Reprinted by permission.

Chapter 5

Separating the Men from the Boys

Few men today can command the sort of power they once enjoyed merely as a result of physical strength. Neither can men today assume, as they once could, that simply by virtue of their prowess at "providing," they are "lord and master" of their households. We can be thankful the day is long gone when the husband held total authority and father always knew best, no matter how wrongheaded he may have been. Some men have accepted these evolutionary changes in regard to the work world, but too many mistakenly attempt to hold onto their outdated authoritarian roles in the home. Some religious fundamentalists have even attempted to reassert patriarchal authority, using scriptural texts as their launching pad. In other cases, men —having lost control over their work lives, having little sense of power outside their homes (except behind the wheel of an auto on the freeway)—seek to wield power at home. Some of the unhappiest families I've worked with

are those where fathers are striving to exercise overt dicta-
torial control. From homes like these, daughters flee into
early marriages or unwed pregnancies, or simply run away.
In a recent year over a quarter of a million children in the
United States ran away from home. The majority of those
reported were female, though it is understood that, significantly, male runaways are not as readily reported to author-
ities. Sons, however, seem to have a tendency simply to
move out of authoritarian home situations as quickly as
possible.

The men responsible for such family problems, in my
experience, are ones who have hemmed themselves in with
fears of what other men might think if they did not act out
their historically scripted role. In so doing, they hand
power over to their peers and suffer a consequent loss of
self-esteem. Feeling unmanned and powerless in the larger
world, they seek to assert authority at home over the "little
woman" and the children. For some, the script they follow
is patterned after their own upbringing, when their parents
had more clearly defined roles and parental authority may
have seemed total. Others act out the script in behavior
patterns resembling those of the schoolyard bully, not
excluding the use of physical power against their wives and
children. Still others maintain an arbitrary control of family
finances, even when the wife is a wage earner.

One common complaint of such men is that "the children don't show me any respect, and she sides with them."
In my experiences with these men in therapy, I find that on
the job they often seem easygoing, even passive, but at
home make exaggerated demands upon their wives and
children to comply with their opinions and desires. One
such client flew into rages if his children so much as

disagreed with him about the relative merits of a given athlete or politician. When his children proved him wrong about the outcome of a particular ball game, he sulked for days and found ways of punishing them. Like the man mentioned earlier, who could feel strong only when his wife was dependent upon him, this man felt his parental authority was threatened by even the slightest difference of opinion. The destructive narrowness of vision of such men is obvious. By their mistaken belief that "authority" over their children is something they can arbitrarily impose, that "respect" is something they can demand, that manly strength is measured only in terms of the visible submission of others to their will, they alienate their wives and children and destroy the foundations of familial love.

Those men who bemoan the loss of "authority" in the home are usually comparing their role to that of their father or grandfather, seeing their "power" or "authority" as emanating from their role as "breadwinner" or "good provider." They leave most actual day-to-day parenting responsibilities to their wives, including visits to the doctor, consultations with teachers, taking the children to church, or tending their wounded knees and egos. They view these and other parental duties as "women's work." Even when the wife is also a wage earner, such men often expect her to continue handling the shopping, cleaning, cooking, and "homemaking" activities without any help from them.

"He doesn't seem to care at all." "He leaves everything up to me." "He's just the oldest boy in the family." Statements like these are commonplace to any therapist dealing with married couples. And just as commonplace is the response of the male: "We've got a nice house, two cars, a trailer [or a boat—sometimes both!]. Those things don't grow on trees. I worked for them." Often this cataloging of possessions is accompanied by an expression of feeling that his efforts go unappreciated and that any further demand upon his energies is unfair.

Those of us men who consider our role as primarily economic, whose identity is rooted in the workplace, who expect our "love" to be self-evident in the fact that we provide the family with consumer goods (though often this would appear to be a by-product of providing ourselves with the ego satisfactions of the status and income competition), are saying very clearly that our place in the lives of our wives and children could very easily be filled by a trust fund. Furthermore, when we invest ourselves so totally in this one aspect of our existence, we skirt the edge of another peril.

During one period of defense cutbacks in California, many engineers who had never previously experienced unemployment flocked to doctors and therapists seeking help with their impotency. More suffered severe depression. One head of a small firm that went broke has not— more than a decade later—returned to work. His wife now supports the family while he remains at home, a semi-alcoholic recluse who refuses to seek therapy.

The inevitable unemployment of retirement likewise holds problems for men who have focused all their energies on their work-role. Often enough, they leave behind the larger part of their social life, which was related to their work. Thrown back on their relationships with their wives and children, such men often find these neglected relationships beyond repair.

Previous male roles and past forms of expressing masculinity simply do not meet the human needs of men and women today. So our highly bureaucratic, technologized, impersonal world demands that men find new ways to express their manliness. There are no panaceas, no "ten easy steps to manhood." However, some among the present generation of men—husbands, fathers, and single men —are working through to new definitions of what manliness is and what it requires of them in our time. More men are becoming receptive to insights that might help them out of the uncomfortable, even painful, places in which they find themselves.

Those who undertake the search often discover that the place to begin is within themselves. Not everyone can take full control of his own life in terms of employment, perhaps, for the majority of us have to earn our keep by working for others. But there is no limit to the changes we can work in our own attitudes toward ourselves and our world. Making the effort to open ourselves up to increased self-awareness also opens up more options in our ways of responding to the people closest to us and to the larger world around us. Even when we move in an impersonal, increasingly bureaucratic and mechanistic environment, our increased self-knowledge can offer us clues to new responses to our personal situation and thus begin the task of changing our personal environment. This re-creation of our lives cannot begin at all, however, unless each of us accepts full responsibility for ourselves. This means taking an honest look at the scripts we may have inherited from a previous generation of parents and teachers. We need, too, to look both at what we are doing to ourselves and others and at the way we are responsible for creating our relationships.

None of us exists in isolation. "No man is an island, entire of itself," John Donne wrote; "every man is a piece of the continent, a part of the main." Our presence in the world is, in fact, our present to the world. Our choices matter. Our style of being ourselves has impact. Our very act of responsibility for creating ourselves as richer, more aware human beings has an effect on those around us. Those men who are committed to the process of discovering themselves and accepting others in a spirit of caring are the true adventurers of the modern world. For if few geographical frontiers confront contemporary men, if the former wilderness is now strapped down by freeways and fast-food establishments, if contemporary voyages of discovery demand not individual initiative and personal courage but billions of dollars and tens of thousands of technicians, there still remains for each man the frontier of his own consciousness, the wilderness of his own feelings. His voyage of discovery into that hitherto unexplored domain of his own being poses a challenge demanding personal initiative and courage.

It is precisely because they have not taken the initiative to sort out their own feelings, have not summoned the courage to try to express those feelings in honest humility to others, that so many men substitute economic contributions for expressions of husbandly or fatherly love. Yet the father who reverences persons, who shows his care for the world of which he is a part and for the persons in his personal world, has no need to demand respect or to worry about his authority. The "authority" of such a man over his children is one which, to use Archbishop Thomas D. Roberts' hallowed phrase, "commends itself in love."[1] Just as the man who wants respect from his children must first of all model it by showing respect to them and other persons, so a man who wishes his counsel to be asked or heeded must first of all demonstrate his loving concern for others' welfare.

It is in these intensely personal family intimacies of husband-wife and parent-child relationships that so many men find their conditioning in the male mystique a barrier to effective relating. The male feels safer away from the mysteries and complexities of interpersonal relationships. For the deepest sense of personal fulfillment, of honest and personal contact with others, calls into play the very range of sensibilities that have been discarded or left underdeveloped by the male mystique. Intimate relating demands a capacity for sensitive listening, an ability to clearly express authentic feelings, a willingness to shed one's armor and to touch and be touched in one's most vulnerable areas of feeling.

Men who do prefer to spend their time with their families rather than with "the boys" will often respond to the "boys' " invitation in a fashion that will be a putdown of their wives and families: "Sorry, the ball and chain insists I spend the weekend with her and the kids." Or "The old lady'd have a fit. I've gotta give her and the kids this Saturday or there'll be hell to pay." For too many American males, to be "one of the boys" means playing along with the notion that family life is just one of those chores that from time to time require attention but are generally a pain. And, as "one of the boys," the man will remain unknown to his friends. The associations formed by males among themselves may be long-lasting, but they are seldom intimate. There is seldom anything approaching a true sharing of personal feelings among males. Recently a client told me he had refused an invitation from the boys by saying, "Thanks a lot, but I'm going to enjoy this weekend with my family. I can't get enough time with them to suit me." During the following week, two of the men who heard him approached him privately to ask what his "secret" was.

A few husbands and fathers have lately broken into print discussing their discovery of the role of "house-husband" or the joy of parenting, of assuming their full share of co-responsibility at home. Immense riches await the married man who sets about the adventure of exploring the territory of his homeland. Recently I sat down with two of my sons and played the *Ungame*, a non-competitive game in which everyone is a winner. In this game, every toss of the dice means that you pick up a card that asks a question such as "If you could be anybody in history, who would it be?" or "In twenty years what would you like to be doing?" Landing on certain spaces lets you ask a question of one of the other participants about one of his or her previous answers. In short, the game builds by sharing insights and oneself with the other participants. And it comes with cards suitable for family, for friends, for a counseling group. Playing this game with my sons was better than the ersatz adventures of the evening movie, for it was an adventure full of surprises as we learned new things about one another and shared ourselves.

I mention this not as a model but as a hint of the sort of spontaneity that is relaxing and also provides a source of mutual enrichment, of deeper familial bonding. Play and leisure activities in our society are often sources of disunity. The television set cuts off dialogue; teenagers have their own concerts and dances; parents have their own evenings out for dinner or bridge. But play and leisure time can be a time when a husband and father can truly relax, join in his wife's and children's lives, enjoy spontaneity, and be at ease with his family.

I dwell upon the paternal or husbandly role only because it is the most important area often neglected by the married majority. Yet we can choose to enrich our families by making a few simple decisions that reorder our priorities in regard to time and energies. Doing so can bring enormous benefits of increased esteem and affection among all family members. It is the mistake of the "boys" in our midst that "power" is expressed by bullying, by authoritarian commands, by threats or the curled fist. But that sort of authority or power lasts only so long as the authority figure is present, and even then it is resented and resisted. A real man, on the other hand, recognizes that the power of love is stronger than death. The person who loves us and who elicits our love in return exercises an influence over us that touches the most hidden recesses of our being. More men who are husbands and fathers need to set about the re-creative task of leaving the "boy" role behind them and striving to become builders of families that are more openly loving and sharing.

But if a shift in attitude can work creative changes for the family man, so too can recognizing his freedom work changes for any male, married or single, young or old. Too many men seem to forget that they are free, can make choices, have options. Despite all the increasingly complicated structure of our society, the individual can still have a say in charting the course of his own life. I think of the dramatic case of the successful corporation attorney who was dissatisfied with his life. After asking himself the hard

questions, he came up with the response that he'd be
happier as a psychologist. His wife had helped him
through college years before. Now her relatives urged her
to resist his "crazy" decision to return to school again. She
herself was reluctant to leave the comfort of their present
situation to return to the slim budget of student days. He
was assaulted by his own family and friends, who told him
he would be letting his wife and family down. And the fact
is, his wife's relatives, his friends and relations might have
been right. He might have discovered it an unwise move.
No doubt any change involves risk, even pain, especially
when it is a change in one's life-style or life's direction.
Against such well-intentioned "common sense," he
decided to return to school. His wife collaborated in his
decision. Today he is one of the country's better known
psychologists and an author credited with helping
thousands of persons to greater happiness. He could have
remained a successful attorney and an unhappy man who
had not realized his full potential.

Most of us don't have such clear-cut choices in the
external world. Freedom is not merely a matter of external
choices; it is an inner quality of spirit. There are men who
were imprisoned (Gandhi, Bonhoeffer, and Martin Luther
King, Jr., spring to mind), who had their liberty removed,
but who never lost their freedom. This sort of freedom
flows from the center of a person who is at home with
himself, who has a sense of his wholeness, his integrity. He
functions without pretense. He does no violence to himself or to others. He has no compulsion to appear to be
someone other than himself. A man can live each day,
savor the joy or confront the sorrow of the moment with

his full faculties. Bonhoeffer, writing of the value of living in the present moment, said:

But is it not characteristic of a man, in contrast with an immature person, that his center of gravity is always where he actually is, and that the longing for the fulfillment of his wishes cannot prevent him from being his whole self, wherever he happens to be?[2]

A man living his life with strength, integrity, and awareness lives with a sense of responsibility toward others. It is a sad truth that too few men live this way, but that does not make it an unattainable goal. There are farmers, bus drivers, bank tellers, men in all walks of life who fit Bonhoeffer's description. It is not the job a man holds that controls his life, but the man himself. Bus travel or visits to the butcher shop or the bank would be more enjoyable experiences if we were met there by free men, men without masks.

Often, American men speak of the pressures under which they work, the pressures of their social life, and so on. Not long ago I said to a friend, "I'm really over-scheduled" and then caught myself. To put it that way made it sound as if my schedule was beyond my control. I quickly rephrased the statement, accepting responsibility for my state of business. I said: "I really overscheduled myself this past week."

When I have a client who says, "I'm feeling this pressure —" my question is "How do you put yourself under such pressure?" I may even ask, "What's your payoff for putting yourself under such pressure?" For some of us, the payoff is that we can then subtly brag about our importance. That necessity to brag puts us among the boys again. A man who is secure enough doesn't need to brag.

Of course, in asking such questions I am simply seeking to get the client to see that he is responsible for creating most of his own pressures. The person in psychotherapy has a head start on many of his peers. He has taken the time to sit down and look at the pressures he is under and find where they came from and what he might do about them. Too many men take pressures for granted, surrender themselves to them, use them as an excuse for not asking themselves the hard questions. They do this because they are insecure, afraid to take that look, and so their anxiety increases the pressures and becomes another part of the self-imposed stress under which they live.

With the shattering of family unity that has taken place in the past few decades, with the collectivization of work and the reduction of its intrinsic value as an outlet for the creative thrust in us, with the quakes rocking the social order generally, no doubt more and more men (and women, too) are going to have to look to themselves for the resources necessary for enjoying life in a fully human way. That so many prefer to flee into the dream and nightmare world of hallucinatory drugs and alcohol only testifies to the upheaval and the sense of alienation that the upheaval is bringing about. But the alternative to such immature behavior is for the male to confront, on the personal level, his need to establish a sense of personal worth and of personal power and personal freedom that will make him strong enough to assert his autonomy in matters concerning his present and his future.

Here, in the battleground at his own center, the heroism of the contemporary man is being tested. His courage is tried, not in confronting some legendary dragon, not in facing up to the bayonet charge of some human opponent outside himself, but in confronting his own human needs, his own fears, facing up to the sharp knife-edge of his own painful feelings of alienation. When he takes those steps that he decides will help him overcome such opponents, when he begins to enunciate and to meet his personal needs, to speak out his fears and thereby rob them of their power, he begins to cauterize his wounds and see them healed through increasing intimacy with his fellow humans.

The capacity to change lies within each of us, whether it means changing our minds about something or working changes in our life-style. Any therapist sees that sort of change being brought about in clients as he or she works with them. Therapy is based upon the reality that people are capable of growth, of turning a painful, debilitating, or depressing situation into a moment of new birth. Instead of seeking to avoid, numb, or deny the pain they feel, more men are beginning to confront it and to use it creatively. I can think of dozens of male clients who in the past few years worked truly marvelous changes in their lives as a result of confronting their own discontent. Instead of the pain of death they experienced the pain of growth. Each had to make some hard decisions; in many cases it meant a change of career, a time of transition full of hardship; in nearly all it meant a redefinition of their own style of being in the world. Some made less dramatic, but just as personally significant, shifts in attitudes. I recall one of them telling me that he had sold his gun collection. "I don't need that any longer," he said. "It was just part of my macho armor." That's the remark of a man who has begun to separate himself from "the boys."

Because the most widely disseminated and accepted notions of manliness are so totally wrongheaded—

"macho" images created by advertisers to sell products—
obviously each man must wrestle with his own redefinition
of his manliness and assert his own dignity as a person. For
many, as I've indicated, that beginning of a new self-esteem
may take place in his own home by his assuming a new role
of service and responsibility, of loving care and openness.
For others it may come through looking at the work they
choose for themselves and seeing whether it contributes to
a personal sense of well-being, to their need for creative
endeavor, to their sense of usefulness to the larger society.

In the last decade, over 20,000 persons moved into
Mendocino County in northern California. According to
one report, they had taken a cut in income amounting to
over two and one-half million dollars annually as they
sought the simpler life-style of that area. Without going
into the impact of the influx on the county and surely
without urging everyone to take to the woods, I believe we
can say that this indicates a direction many men are taking.
Other rural areas and small towns report similar newcom-
ers. Many of these people are seeing that the route to their
personal salvation, the way to increase their self-esteem and
to develop a life-style that enhances their dignity, does not
lie in having consumer products or occupational status. It
lies, rather, in cutting back on working for material goods,
in laying aside the competitive striving for job titles and
seeking out more satisfying, less tension-filled, more personally rewarding work—in short, in practicing a simpler
life-style. Many others do not change jobs, but themselves.
By working to make themselves more human in the context of their work, they bring a humanizing influence to
that work.

That humanizing influence, that care for others and for the earth itself as our human home, is a major challenge confronting men and demanding their attention. So far, too few men have taken this message to heart, accepted it personally. In one month, drivers in California burned up nearly a billion gallons of gas. This record fuel consumption occurred in spite of billboards and television spots urging us to conserve energy. Yet our acceptance of social responsibility as men will have to come in terms of simplifying our life-style. The goods of the earth are at stake, as is the future of all human beings. The reckless consumers are the boys in our midst who live as if there were no tomorrow. They've not accepted adult manly responsibility for their share in creating the future. Part of the reason why they've not done so is that the urgings for conservation and care of creation run counter to their upbringing that tells them that conspicuous consumption of goods is a way of displaying power and manly success.

Most men who have opted for a simpler life-style report they now enjoy a greater freedom. They experience less tension, less anxiety about the future. Because such simplification flows from the inner man outward, those men who do make such changes in their goals usually have already shifted their emphasis from externals to the more rewarding essentials of life. Taking responsibility for the quality of their lives, something boys aren't mature enough to do even when the boys are fifty or sixty, such men usually exercise their autonomy to bring greater harmony and inner calm to themselves. They experience greater ease, and their calm strength permeates all their relationships. Using the energy they formerly spent on creating a power base, they now work to build up bonds of affection and goodwill with those around them, putting their energies into causes they feel will benefit the world at large. The satisfactions brought to such men by their personal relationships, by their occupational efforts, and by their volunteer efforts are beyond price. One of those satisfactions is that they do less questioning of their own personhood as men, of their own sense of strength, for they exercise that strength each day in ways that count the most.

Obviously, we can't bring about a redefinition of manliness in our time by requisitioning it. Who could have told St. Francis of Assisi beforehand that he would become one of the most beloved, inspirational, and strongest men in the world by refusing to enter his father's business and by going about town begging for food? No, each of us has his own way to work in the world, his own calling. But to find that way we must heed the call as it expresses itself in us.

This chapter has given me occasion to think about the great men I've been privileged to know. Some of them are great in the eyes of the world, very well known, but I will not embarrass them by using their names here. Some are not well known beyond the circle of their family and friends. I tried to come to terms with what was common to each of these men who truly deserve the title of men.

All of them had the qualities I've been talking about: the willingness to face themselves honestly and to admit that there were times when it was difficult to face themselves. All put various spiritual, ethical, or human values ahead of material things, though for some the material things came their way as a result of their work. But all of them had discovered and dedicated themselves to their work. That is, they had some passionate involvement or involvements that tapped their creative energies, involvements that did not pay the bills but that these men supported by jobs of various sorts. Whether those involvements were ideological, artistic, political, or social, all of them were aimed at improving the human condition. Sometimes the involvements demanded great personal risk: taking an unpopular stand, losing a job, even facing death. Nearly all the involvements were rooted in the conviction that every human being is a miracle. Each of these men is a man of great vitality, his labors not draining his energies but seeming always to bring new energies bubbling up. In this vitality these men witness to the truth of the paradox that he who loses his life saves it.

One of them, now over seventy years old, just began a new teaching stint. Really, it is an old teaching post, one he lost twenty-seven years ago because he refused to go against his conscience. Now the Supreme Court and the State Legislature have said he was right in his very unpopular stand. Though he is plagued with an illness that grows progressively more burdensome, his vitality is prodigious, as is his constant wonder at the world.

All these great men share that sense of wonder, of reverence for the gift of life itself. It is that very sense of wonder and of reverence that makes them all men of good humor and of peace. They have the courage to be themselves, and that means they are open to the child in themselves, able to play and to laugh freely as well as to speak their minds openly. Even the wealthiest among them lives simply, having no need to seek to impress anyone else by outward symbols. All of them share the courage to be alive, fully alive, and open to growth in those around them.

I said earlier that it is hard to requisition manliness, to write out a prescription for it that we can then set out to fill, but as I thought of friends who fit the title of man as I describe it, it seems to me that the above-mentioned traits are essential, though they are of course modified by each of the unique personalities I know. There is not a whiner or complainer in the lot, despite the fact that at least two of these men suffer severe physical health problems and all have suffered their share, if not more than their share, of growing pains. Indeed, in some ways because they are so open to the sufferings of others, they seem to have taken on themselves the burdens of many; but not one puts on a martyr's face or displays his old war wounds to prove his heroism.

Yes, separating the men from the boys comes down to describing a man as one who is willing to look the truth in the face—the truth about himself and about the world—and to seek beauty and goodness in his life, to stretch for the full ecstasy of living by striving to be all that he can be, using his talents to the utmost and, while being serious in his efforts and capable of crying real tears at the sufferings of others, still maintaining that redeeming sense of play that reveals his joy in life.

All these men are also religious in the most profound sense of that term. That is, they are aware of their dependency upon the Source of their existence. They share an insight into the redemptive value of suffering, and they share a profound hope, a confidence that even should their best efforts seem to fail for the moment, such efforts have not been wasted but in the Divine Economy are caught up and will one day be seen as part of the overall work of creating the new earth. They have what the ancients called "piety," that basic sense of reverence for their heritage, for their Creator, for their fellow creatures, and for all the beauties of the earth. Qualities such as these, it seems to me, enable such persons to take the risks and face the challenges that ultimately separate the men from the boys.

But such qualities are not gifts lavished on only a few. Each of us can attain them. They are part of our own basic humanity. All that is required of us is to accept responsibility for those choices that work to create ourselves and our world. If our age doesn't demand death-defying acts as assertions of manliness, it does require life-enhancing activities. And those choices can often require incredible courage.

Recently at a public lecture a man asked me about the "disparity" between various aspects of a man's life, between the roles he was called upon to play at work, at home, as child to his parents, as parent to his child, and also about the various conflicting demands upon him. My response was that creating ourselves involves precisely that task of working against compartmentalization, against role-playing and toward the integration of our persons so that we no longer feel split up or alienated from our true selves, but instead experience that sense of integrity we call wholeness. To pilgrim forth in that direction is to move toward the goal of experiencing more the joy of life.

Instead of the low kind of play that engages so much of our attention, such as oneupmanship over our peers, we might turn to what Harmon Bro has called "high play."[3] We then step into that realm in which we, in a sense, risk our lives daily by putting ourselves on the line in faith, hope, and love. For it is in confronting my daily tasks, in dealing with this person before me now, in making this decision about myself, or that one about where I am going, that each of us is at work shaping ourself and our future. And that is the process whereby the boys are separated out, left behind by the men who volunteer themselves for this task.

Reflection/Discussion Questions

1.   What do "the boys" do together in your community?

2.   What does a father have to give up to show caring to his children? What does he gain?

3.   What does a husband have to give up to show caring to his partner? What does he gain?

4.   In what ways do you put yourself under pressure?

5.   In what directions would you like to grow as a person?

6.   How, specifically, could you simplify your life-style and enhance your enjoyment of life?

7.   What involvements or commitments do you have that help create a better world?

Notes

1.   *Black Popes—Authority: Its Use and Abuse* (London: Longmans, Green, 1954).

2. Quoted in William Kuhns, *In Pursuit of Dietrich Bonhoeffer* (Dayton, Ohio: Pflaum Press, 1967), p. 134.

3. *High Play* (New York: Coward McCann, 1970).

Chapter 6

Passion, Poetry, and Potency

In a paper delivered as the keynote address at a national convention of psychologists, Dr. Pierre Mornell pointed out that an increasing number of marriages are failing because of passive-dependent husbands. Dr. Mornell described an evening at home with such a man:

He arrives around 7:00 P.M. exhausted from a day at the office. He has usually spent his day dealing with people and their problems and he's had it up to his eyeballs. He wants to hide, to withdraw, retreat from everyone—including (or especially) his family. He has a drink or two, reads the newspaper, wolfs down his dinner paying only token attention to his wife, maybe a little more to the kids, and withdraws behind television's Monday Night Football game or Tuesday night's movies. Remaining glued to the set through the 11:00 P.M. news, he usually comes to bed with his wife already asleep.[1]

Dr. Mornell's scenario goes on to point out that as this sort
of behavior causes home life to deteriorate further and this
man's wife to express dissatisfaction, he may take to coming home later and later. He may start an affair, or the
passive man may take three stiff drinks before dinner and a
bottle of wine with dinner, and end up dozing off on the
couch in a neat avoidance of any demands for sexual
gymnastics or marital intimacy.

Naturally, such behavior causes his wife to make more
insistent demands for attention or tenderness—or just plain
help with the children—and that furthers his retreat. "She
feels more pressured," Mornell described, "becomes abu-
sive. He retreats further. She becomes hysterical and
bitchy." Then she becomes, in the face of his passivity,
what Mornell calls a "wild, wild woman."

One recently divorced woman client of mine, typical of
others, gave a different ending to Mornell's script:

I'd be expected to do the shopping on the way home
from my own work. I prepared dinner while he
watched T.V. and soothed his nerves with a drink.
He'd nap in front of the set while I cleaned up after
dinner, bathed the children, read to them, tucked
them in for the night. Then I'd shower and get in bed
with a book to relax—and he'd come in raring to go
for sex. When I said I needed some time to unwind
and get in the mood, he'd get angry and call me frigid!

Often the frustrated woman will express her resentment by
demanding that her husband do more around the house.
Should the passive man do the dishes, pick up his own
clothes or do other things to "pacify" her, this often simply
makes her wilder. Mornell comments: "I think she keeps
goading her husband because unconsciously she is

threatened by the power she is developing over him." The women married to such men describe their husbands to Mornell as "weak, immature, absent, ineffectual, indifferent, uninvolved, inactive, uncaring or—another child needing care." This last comment parallels my own previously mentioned experience of hearing many wives speak disparagingly of their husbands as "the oldest boy in the family."

For many such passive-dependent husbands, sexual activity has decreased drastically, and impotence or premature ejaculation has become symptomatic. For others, the sexual expression of their relationship has become perfunctory, a sort of sleeping pill—taken with about as little pleasure. "We have been so crippled by the American myth about machoism [sic] and strength and what it means to be a fulfilled male," actress Jane Fonda commented, "that many men can't function with the sensitivity and generosity that is needed to make a good lover—a complete human being, man or woman."[2] Some men, indeed, respond with increasingly compulsive behavior in regard to sex as a reassurance of their masculinity. One wife commented:

George demanded more and more sex. Any time we were alone, he'd grab for me. I took to avoiding him, by being "too busy." If I awakened at night, he'd immediately make sexual advances. I liked it when we used to make love, but having sex on his demand, no matter how I felt, was not lovemaking.

One client's husband literally would race home at lunch or in mid-afternoon for a "quickie." Once, when he found some of his wife's friends in the house and the cleaning lady in the bedroom, he insisted on doing it on the bathroom floor. Her protests were of no avail at these times. He insisted it was a manifestation of his great love for her!

"I felt raped more than loved. When I threatened to leave,
he talked of suicide." Unable to educate him, she divorced
him.

Revelatory for any man is a book like Ingrid Bengis's
remarkable personal account of her experiences of love,
hate and sex, *Combat in the Erogenous Zone.*

What I wanted was to discover men who were passionate, but also understood restraint; men who were
sexually competent but capable of choosing whom to
be competent with; men who realized from something within themselves (not something imposed
upon them) that mind, body, and spirit need to be
integrated before body can involve itself deeply; men
who could say yes and no; men for whom such a
choice really exists. To me, that is what a man is, a
person with passions who is also capable of making
free and responsible choices.[3]

Precisely because the author had not yet met men who
could live up to that description—and had met too many of
the other variety—the words are found in a section titled
"Man-Hating."

Thus we return to the theme of the universal need to
integrate body and spirit. We all must take upon ourselves
the creative responsibility for bridging the gap between our
convictions and our actions, between our felt needs and
our expressed desires.

A man has a great need to shed his armor, to step out of
the stereotypical and outmoded role the male mystique has
imposed upon him since his earlier years. A greater sense of
accomplishment in his work, greater freedom to discover
himself, will result. Sometimes the process of growth is
triggered by his recognizing that a man still has the power

of choice and that the touchstone of manliness today consists of displaying the courage to become what his best instincts and deepest feelings are prompting him to be. Even very small personal decisions involving his coming to terms with himself will have ramifications in his life-style and will therefore become a part of the redeeming energy our society so drastically needs.

Once again we need to look at our choices. The ability to say a firm yes or no, whether to ourselves, to others, or to social pressures, is the basic strength of the mature human being. We have mentioned a few of those basic choices in previous chapters. Earlier, too, we made the point that the mature man is a man passionately involved, intensely concerned with persons, with life, with what he has chosen as his "work"—which we distinguished from his job even though the two can be one and the same.

In our era we have witnessed a deterioration, even a collapse, of the important role work used to play in helping a man appreciate his strength and express himself creatively. The technologizing of jobs, the depersonalization of much of the workaday world, leaves many with a sense of depletion, disappointment, even unhappiness. At the same time, for many the political world has grown too complex. Our recent experiences of it—from assassinations to corruption in high places, to the corrupters making millions on their crimes—have turned many away from this important area of involvement, away from passionate interest and creative expression. Add to this the upheaval of religious and moral and social values—where nothing seems stable anymore—and we have set the stage for the most bizarre expressions of sexuality.

It ought not surprise us that if their job is meaningless, many seek meaning off the job, in recreational pursuits. Some expect cheap eroticism to offer a sense of "life." Because they have little control over public life and therefore feel unimportant there, some seek a sense of "freedom" or importance, however fleeting, in sexual escapades. If there is no longer an easy confidence about accepted standards, some reason for them, then why follow the more difficult path of having any standards at all? Why not seek personal pleasure wherever it may be found?

It is no accident that the age that has seen the dislocations we've outlined has also seen an enormous increase of emphasis on sexual expressions in the genital sense, and particularly emphasis on the pursuit of sexual gratification as an end in itself. Thus we have both the explosion of the pornography industry and the proliferation of texts that seek to teach people the proper ways to manipulate one another for sexual pleasure.

Hard-core pornography, however, which all agree feeds on the unreality of male fantasies, is by definition anti-erotic. Pornography is hard, while true eroticism means softness and tender caring. One woman client related that she had accompanied her husband to a nightclub that showed so-called "erotic" films.

> We wanted to see what they were all about. They were
> the opposite of erotic. My husband and I had a good
> relationship sexually until then. Those films affected
> me so that I was unable to enjoy, really didn't want,
> sex for weeks. They were anti-sex. They made it
> repulsive.

Similarly, the texts that devote themselves to the manipulation of genitals tend to lead people down the path of depersonalizing the sexual act, reducing it to a matter of mere technique. This is why a woman like Bengis can observe that the passionate man would be one who would realize "that mind, body and spirit need to be integrated before body can involve itself deeply."[4] That is the truth the manuals leave out, and it is a critical truth, at the core of the problem of male sexuality today. The search for pleasure as pleasure alone—and pornography is the pleasure of the passive male—is doomed. For pleasure alone does not meet the needs of the fully grown person. Indeed, so quickly does pleasure of this sort cease to please that the pleasure-seeker slides rapidly into a search for variety, for promiscuity, and ends up frantically grasping for a handhold on the edge of despair.

In pornography there is no poetry, no tenderness, no expression of the spirit or of personal involvement. On the other hand, the truly erotic issues forth in poetry. The truly erotic is rooted in the union of two loving persons. The sexual mechanic's manuals overlook this essential truth: that the magic, the power, the true potency—the potential of that moment when two persons embrace—flows out of the mystery of their personal relationship. When that relationship is impoverished, when they are using each other solely as instruments of pleasure, then they know the letdown of separation, of isolation, for the act does not symbolize for them a deeper unity, a communion. It does not renew or re-create them in love. "I've never experienced sex as you describe it here," one former client commented upon reading this, "yet I believe it can be that. I want to experience sexual expression in this way. When I do, I'll know the difference between the gymnastics of my former husband and true sharing in sexual intimacy."

Some men seek "adventure" in the sexual realm, whether it is the adventure of having an affair or the adventure of a new "conquest" of some woman. This sort of "adventure" is a mark of the restlessness of contemporary men. Most often, in my opinion, this behavior marks a man's further attempt to escape confronting himself. Worse, it is exploitive, for he is using other persons as a means of bolstering his faltering confidence in his masculinity. Despite all the current media emphasis upon sexual matters, from the pornographic film to the talk-show sexologist, and for all the license we know exists, a terrible confusion remains about what constitutes effective sexual functioning. In fact, as is by now obvious, pornographic material and exploitive behavior flow out of that confusion even as they serve to increase it. All too much of our culture portrays sexual activity as something segregated from the rest of our being. This is so whether sexual arousal is being used to sell us products or is the graphic display of genital activity in magazines or on movie screens. Sexual activity (we cannot call it erotic loving) is treated as an autonomous activity, a one-night stand engaged in to alleviate a boring weekend. The belief that sexual activity has a reality unconnected with the rest of our being is one of the cruelest untruths of our time. That sexual heresy is the source of much personal suffering in those who accept it, and it causes much of the marital conflict therapists are asked to resolve.

Our appreciation of our sexuality is intimately linked to our appreciation of our identity. The expression of ourselves sexually is either enriched or impoverished by our view of ourselves. A healthy sexual life is the mark of an integrated personality. The more we come to terms with our own inner experiences, the more we can express ourselves freely—that is, with choice—as sexual beings. The rapist, for example, is following an unexamined compulsion, giving vent to hostility, anger, or some other nonerotic impulse. The Don Juan, whose efforts are constantly directed toward making a new conquest, is seeking reassurance for himself about his masculinity. But he does not gain reassurance that way, or he would not continue the search.

Healthy sexual expression, the transports of passion, and the sense of a fulfilling union come to the man whose erotic activities take place in the context of tenderness, desire, and affection. Healthy sexuality finds expression as a free gift, not as a compulsion, and arises out of the desire to give and receive pleasure in union with the beloved.

What we do cannot be separated from who we are. And thus I cannot generously give myself to my beloved if I am not a generous person. I cannot express tenderness in my love relationship if I am—because of my miseducation in the male mystique—afraid of showing tenderness. My sexual lovemaking cannot be a total communication of myself if I am unwilling to give myself away in intimate sharing.

The more aware I become of my own inner experience of myself and my life, the more unafraid I am to share that experience. The more I am able to grow in a healthy appreciation of my manliness and to share that manliness, the less likely I am to choose to be locked into living some inauthentic stereotyped role.

This appreciation of the integral nature of our sexuality and of our personal growth in appreciation of ourselves as sexed persons does not come easily. We Americans are

notorious "problem-solvers." Our technological civilization is built upon our genius at tackling enormous technical problems. We usually do so by breaking them down
into their component parts and working out solutions to
each part. Then we put the whole together and end up with
a man on the moon or with Mariner voyaging on a two-
year trip to Jupiter. The matter of human sexuality, of the
masculine-feminine relationship, of getting to know ourselves and becoming more human, however, is not a problem to be solved that way. Despite the neatly packaged
answers to sex problems that we read in Dear Abby or
Playboy Advisor or Helen Gurley Brown, every couple
must work out its own solutions.

It is possible to view the heavy emphasis upon sexual
gratification in our time less as a sign of our corruption as a
civilization and more as a manifestation of persons looking
for intimacy, for communion, for connectedness with one
another, for relatedness. It is unfortunate that so many,
because of the current moral confusion, are choosing genital activity as a solution to their problem, even as an end in
itself. At its best, genital activity is an expression of relatedness, of intimacy, of unity already achieved. When it is that,
then it also serves to further that relatedness, that intimacy,
that unity. No amount of mechanical tinkering or increase
in quantity or variety of sexual partners can compensate for
the lack of such relatedness between persons.

While most would agree that we live in a sex-saturated
society, we need to look at the other side of the picture.
There are large numbers of married couples in this society
whose sexual activity has come to a standstill or is nonexistent or nearly so. There are enough unconsummated
marriages in our society to have occasioned an article and a

book about them.[5] There are numerous marriages in which
the male has simply given up because of the enormous
demands his performance mystique and his macho concept
have placed on him. For these persons, as well as for the
single men who are in the dark about what their masculinity means today, the answers will not be found in "Pent-
house Forum" or "Sexology."

The answer will be found in taking the time to face
fearlessly the hard questions of their personal identity:
What do I really want from myself in life? What do I want
to give to life? Who am I? What is my destiny? These are
basically religious questions, questions of my relatedness to
my Creator and to fellow creatures. They are questions
about values, about what is important to me. They are life-
and-death questions.

Redbook magazine once surveyed its readers and came up
with the "astonishing" (to *Redbook* editors) discovery that
religious married women enjoyed sexual lovemaking more
and reported more orgasmic joy in it than did those who
identified themselves as non-churchgoing, and more than
single women. A few months later it had an article supposedly interpreting this finding. The essence of the "interpre-
tation" was that the churches had, of late, become more
liberal in their view of sex. How that accounted for the
lack of liberality among the non-churchgoing or single
women, I don't know. The "explanation" missed the point.
The survey ought to have surprised no one because: 1) the
married women are in a committed relationship; that is,
they feel secure in the relationship and able to "give themselves away" and 2) they are religious; that is, they have an
integrated view of themselves as children of God, persons
who can let themselves go in trust and confidence.

I mention that survey about women, though our subject is men, because I believe it has transference value. The man who has answered the fundamental questions about his life's meaning, who has a sense of his personal identity as one whose personal actions matter, and who comprehends his responsibility toward himself and others in the love-relationship described in the Gospels is a man also freed to be himself, a man open to the revelations of divine love in his life and willing to give of that love to others.

The home does remain an area still basically free of intrusion by the state and not yet merged into a conglomerate. The home remains a private domain, and its emotional quality is very much the creation of the co-responsible parents. For all the grim statistics about divorce in our society, over one million couples have in the past nine years participated in Marriage Encounters. The Marriage Encounter is a forty-four-hour experience in which husbands and wives meet each other in a positive setting and are taught some methods of communication.[6] These Encounters are held under Catholic, Protestant, and Jewish auspices. The exercises are strictly for the husband-wife and are conducted in private by them. Spouses learn to communicate with each other in a loving way, to have a more authentic sharing than most have ever experienced in their relationship. The great majority come away truly enriched, holding hands, radiating a new joy and increased pleasure. Despite such testimonials, I know couples who refuse invitations to go on such a weekend—and in every case that has come to my attention it is the husband who doesn't wish to attend.

Here again we find a man who, though given the possibility of new life, of increased passion and, yes, poetry, in his life, of enhanced potency, greater energy in his marriage, loses his nerve. What is his fear? I believe it is the fear we mentioned in the first chapter: the fear of self-disclosure, the fear of true intimacy with another, even with one's own spouse. A man who perhaps won the Silver Star for gallantry in action, a man who would bloody your nose if you called him a coward, turns his back upon an opportunity to enhance his marriage because he fears revealing himself to his wife.

I don't mean to make the Marriage Encounter a litmus-paper test of true manliness but only to use it as an example of a contemporary opportunity that is sometimes refused by a male because he dreads being asked to get in touch with his feelings and to express them to someone he says he loves and who loves him.

Plato said, "The life which is unexamined is not worth living." To live unexamined lives is becoming increasingly intolerable for us men, married or single. The struggle for meaning in our lives, the search for authenticity, is one of the hallmarks of this confused era. It is a confusing picture, but paradoxically it signals the desire of many to find a way out of the confusion. All around us are cults, new religions, human-potential centers, psychological pundits, gurus, commanding the attention of many. Oftentimes they promulgate new myths or new errors about men and women. But while the time is not without its peril, I believe it signals hope. It announces that more and more persons in our midst are searching for answers to the right questions. That should give us a basis for optimism about the future. The more I take care of my own hang-ups, resolve my inner conflicts, the more time and energy I have to handle the world outside me—and that includes you.

The man-woman struggle itself is working toward a redefinition of the relationship of the sexes.

As more men and women are finding that isolating sexual activity from the context of tenderness and affection and a commitment to the partner's good is a losing proposition, we find them seeking to place that sort of activity back into its full human context. Women have taken the lead in this endeavor, but increasing numbers of men are opening themselves up to the greater joy inherent in such an attempt.

The basic gender differences between men and women remain: the irreducible biological differences that men can impregnate and women can menstruate, become pregnant, and lactate. No longer, however, can anyone assume that man means stronger, woman, weaker; that man means superior, woman, inferior; that man spells breadwinner, woman, homemaker; or man, active, woman, passive.

If mere males still tend to look upon their wives and other women as if they were of a different species, true men are accepting of them as fellow human beings involved in the common task of civilizing the world, making it more of a home for us all. This means that those who aspire to the title of man today are involved in the collaborative task of homemaking on the domestic level, accepting co-responsiblity for parenting and housework. While the "boy" would leave this to "mother" and the male would find it a threat to his insecure hold on his sexual role, the man is secure enough in his identity to know that shouldering his share of these responsibilities is but another exercise of his talents in the service of creating the new earth for which we yearn.

While the "boy" looks to the woman in his life to provide him with nurture and the "male" rages against any sensitivity in himself as a sign of weakness, the man unashamedly cultivates his self-awareness and seeks to develop his aesthetic and spiritual qualities as well as his physical strengths. Not only does he not feel threatened by the flow of his own tears; he is strong enough to know that it is truly in our vulnerabilities, not in our so-called "successes," that we meet one another.

Indeed, one of the by-products of the women's movement is that it has helped to "liberate the woman in every man," as someone has commented. If by "woman" in that context we mean the softer aspects, then that is so. Men— unlike the "boys" and the "males" in our midst—have the ability to be gentle, nurturing, tender, openly receptive to the pain of others.

Eschewing the all-too-abundant phony substitutes for relating, refusing either to rage impotently against the inner alienation he feels or to whine for someone to care for him, the man is aware of how the weaker, more fragile aspects of human life require his manly assistance, his protective strength, his nurture and caring. He responds by asserting his will against such things as environmental pollution, civic corruption, world hunger, the oppression of the aged —all the foes that lurk in the wilderness of today's world. He is aware that even the general moral drift, the social dislocations, the deterioration of educational and public standards, are ills susceptible to the influence of individual persons passionately committed to goals that are beyond the petty standards of status and income.

Such a man does not retire from his job to become a
"useless" being getting "underfoot" all day in the house-
hold that is his wife's domain—the plaint of so many wives
of retirees ("What will I do with him sitting around the
house all day, complaining?"). His work is never done, and
the tasks of keeping house are not foreign to him.

Recently I asked the women in one of my lecture audi-
ences for a definition of sex appeal: "What is a sexy man?"
The descriptive phrases that came forth had little to do
with Robert Redford's eyes or Sylvester Stallone's phy-
sique. Rather there were phrases like "caring and sharing,"
"concerned about people," "excited about life in general,"
"lots of energy—you know, vital, involved," "tender,"
"open," "creative and committed," "committed to princi-
ples, not wishy-washy," "sensitive to others," "self-assured,
able to relax or work, to laugh at himself and to cry at
beautiful or sad things."

Not long ago a young mother of four came to me.
Through her tears she informed me that she was going to
divorce her husband and had already made an appointment
with an attorney. Her husband had for a long while
evidenced great jealousy over the time she gave the children. He seemed perpetually angry and ruined nearly every
dinner by some outburst at the children over spilled milk or
food left on the plate. All signs of affection had ceased
except for occasional "lovemaking" episodes "which are
over in twenty minutes or less and which I endure because
otherwise he just gets angrier, but I no longer enjoy sex
with him." The evening before she had made her appointment with me, he had "called me names in front of the
children, at the dinner table, and when my daughter said he

shouldn't talk that way he shouted that now I had turned the children against him, too."

I asked her if she had told him of her decision. She said she hadn't, fearing his anger. I asked if she had invited him to come in to therapy. She hadn't because she "knew he'd say no." I suggested to her that she take the risk of having a quiet conversation with him, telling him only of her own feelings and of the fact that she had been to see me and was going to see an attorney because, unless he changed, she would have to leave him for her sake and the sake of the children. I urged her to speak only of her own feelings, not of his behavior, and of her wanting him as her husband but of her inability to live in that emotional climate. Then she was to invite him into counseling with her.

To her surprise, he not only listened; he cried at the thought of losing her. He accepted her invitation to come to the next appointment with her. In the meantime they talked as they had not talked in years. When they arrived together, he was open to any help I might offer him to heal the wounds he had caused. Most of them were caused by his "boy" behavior at having lost her as his "mother" and by his attempts to find a new position in the family constellation—attempts based upon the "male mystique" of belligerent behavior meant to show his strength.

Fortunately, he was very cooperative. Within six sessions, their relationship was on an entirely new plane: that of honest sharing, of romantic dinners out, of walks on the beach and family outings. "I have one regret," he said in the final session: "that I wasted so many years and caused so much pain before I found myself."

As more males take steps to come to terms with their total being-in-the-world, as they begin to tap their potential to create themselves as fully human beings, eschewing the phony symbols of masculinity, the pursuit of the goddesses of status and material success, and start to take the risks of self-discovery, of self-disclosure, of making truly loving commitments, of accepting responsibility not only for creating themselves but for co-creating the world in which they live (both the microcosm of the family and the macrocosm of the earth), then we will begin to appreciate the exciting age in which we live. We will then see this as a time when, for all the messy struggles and pains of birthing, men began to realize their full stature and knew the heady experience that is the passion of men fully alive, the poetry of God's creation, and the potency of creative loving.

Reflection/Discussion Questions

1.   After reading this book, what questions do you feel are the crucial ones to ask about your own life? List them below.

a.

b.

c.

2. Ask your wife, or a significant woman friend, to read this book and discuss with you the points she found most helpful in understanding you.

Notes

1. Christopher Reed, "Passive Men and Wild Women," *Des Moines Register*, May 10, 1977. An advance report on Dr. Pierre Mornell's keynote address before the National Convention of Psychologists in San Francisco.

2. Quoted in "Hue and Cry" column of "This World" section of the *San Francisco Chronicle*, April 30, 1978, p. 20.

3. Ingrid Bengis, *Combat in the Erogenous Zone* (New York: Bantam Books, 1972), p. 70.

4. Ibid.

5. See Vance Packard, *The Sexual Wilderness* (New York: David McKay, 1968), p. 271.

6. See Don Demarest and Jerry and Marilyn Sexton, *Marriage Encounter: A Guide for Sharing* (New York: Carillon Books, 1978).

Bibliography

Barbeau, Clayton. *The Art of Loving.* Cincinnati: St. Anthony's Messenger Tapes, 1976.

Barbeau, Clayton. *Creative Marriage: The Middle Years.* New York: Seabury Press, 1976. Now available as *Joy of Marriage.* Minneapolis: Winston Press, 1979.

Bengis, Ingrid. *Combat in the Erogenous Zone.* New York: Bantam Books, 1972.

Blood, Robert O., and Wolfe, Donald M. *Husbands and Wives: The Dynamics of Married Living.* New York: Free Press, 1960.

Bro, Harmon H., Ph.D. *High Play.* New York: Coward McCann, 1970.

Demarest, Don, and Sexton, Jerry and Marilyn. *Marriage Encounter: A Guide for Sharing.* New York: Carillon Books, 1978.

Dizard, Jan E. "The Price of Success." *The Future of the Family.* Edited by Louise Kapp Howe. New York: Simon & Schuster, 1972.

Dizard, Jan. E. *Social Change in the Family.* Chicago: Community and Family Study Center, University of Chicago, 1968.

Farrell, Warren. *The Liberated Man.* New York: Bantam Books, 1975.

Fasteau, Marc. *The Male Machine.* New York: McGraw-Hill, 1974.

Ferguson, Charles W. *The Male Attitude.* Boston: Little, Brown, 1966.

Fitzgerald, F. Scott. *The Crack-Up.* Edited by Edmund Wilson. New York: New Directions, 1945.

Gagnon, John H. "The Passing of the Dominant Husband-Father," *Impact of Science on Society* 21, No. 8 (1971), 21-30.

Goldberg, Herb, Ph.D. *The Hazards of Being Male.* New York: Signet Books, 1976.

"Half of Marital Problems Caused by Adultery." *Des Moines Register,* April 11, 1977.

"Hue and Cry" column of "This World" section, *San Francisco Chronicle.* April 30, 1978, p. 20.

Jourard, Sidney. *The Transparent Self.* New York: Van Nostrand, 1964.

Korda, Michael. *Power: How to Get It—How to Use It.* New York: Random House, 1975.

Kuhns, William. *In Pursuit of Dietrich Bonhoeffer.* Dayton, Ohio: Pflaum Press, 1967.

LeShan, Eda. *The Wonderful Crisis of Middle Age.* New York: Warner Paperback Library, 1973.

Lewis, Michael. "Parents and Children: Sex Role Development." *School Review* 80 (1972).

Mailer, Norman. "The Time of Her Time." *Advertisements for Myself.* New York: Signet Books, 1960, pp. 427-451.

Miller, H.P. *Rich Man, Poor Man.* New York: Crowell, 1964.

Milner, Esther, Ph.D. *The Failure of Success.* St. Louis, Mo.: Warren H. Green, 1968.

Packard, Vance. *A Nation of Strangers.* New York: Pocket Books, 1974.

Packard, Vance. *The Sexual Wilderness.* New York: David
McKay, 1968.

Pleck, Joseph, and Sawyer, Jack. *Men and Masculinity.*
Englewood Cliffs, N.J.: Prentice-Hall, Spectrum Books,
1974.

Psychology Today 10, No. 8 (January 1977).

Reed, Christopher. "Passive Men and Wild Women." *Des
Moines Register,* May 10, 1977.

Roberts, Thomas D. *Black Popes—Authority: Its Use and
Abuse.* London: Longmans, Green, 1954.

Rosenzweig, Saul. "Sexual Autonomy as an Evolutionary
Attainment, Anticipating Proceptive Sex Choice and Idi-
odynamic Bisexuality." *Contemporary Sexual Behavior:
Critical Issues in the 1970's.* Edited by Joseph Zubin and
John Money. Baltimore and London: Johns Hopkins
University Press, 1973.